# Ring Revelations

Unraveling the Stories of Boxing's Past, Present, and Future

**Bruce Miller**

**Ring Revelations: Unraveling the Mysteries of Boxing's Past, Present, and Future,** Copyright © 2024, Bruce Miller. All rights reserved. No part of this book may be reproduced or transmitted in any form or by any means, electronic or mechanical, including photocopying, recording, or by any information storage and retrieval system, without written permission from the author and publisher, except for brief quotations as would be used in a review.

Cover by King of Designer. Images are from creative commons except where indicated. Every effort is made to make the information in this book be current but changes as time passes due to boxing schedules and results.

ISBN 978-1-99-104870-7 Paperback B&W

ISBN 978-1-99-104871-4 Paperback Color

*Ring Revelations*
*Unraveling the Mysteries of Boxing's Past, Present, and Future*

*"You don't have to be in a boxing ring to be a great fighter. As long as you are true to yourself, you will succeed in your fight for that in which you believe."*

-- **Muhammad Ali**

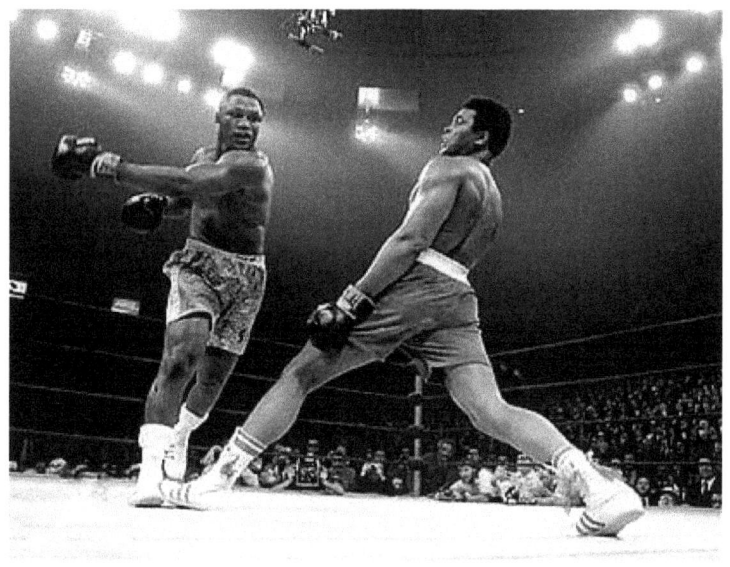

*Muhammad Ali vs. Joe Frazier*

*"Man. I've been through a lot as a kid. But at the same time that upbringing just made me stronger and made me more determined to make it out of where I made it out from and just fight extra hard to not go back."*

**-- Terence "Bud" Crawford.** An impressive career record of 40 wins and no losses, 31 of which came by way of knockout. *Ring Magazine* ranked Crawford as the top boxer in the world in their August 2023 issue, recognizing his historic feat in 2017 as the first boxer to hold the WBA, WBC, WBO, and IBF lightweight championships simultaneously -- a distinction spanning the decade from 2010 through 2020.

Crawford moved up to the welterweight division in 2018. That year, he defeated Jeff Horn to capture the WBO welterweight championship. In early 2023, Crawford defeated Errol Spence Jr., becoming the first male fighter in history to hold undisputed championships in two different weight classes - cementing his place among the all-time greats in the sport. In 2023 the IBF stripped him of his IBF Championship due to his inability (schedule issues) to fight Jaron 'Boots' Ennis.

Crawford began boxing at age seven. When asked about growing up, he got tough by the inner-city streets of north Omaha, where lack of opportunities and crime dominated.

He was shot in the head after a street dice game and believes he survived because the car window slowed the bullet -- underscoring that life was always difficult and nothing came easy. He was never simply given anything and had to work for rewards or achieve them through his own efforts. *"Either I had to work for it or I had to do something good for it. It was never, 'You can have this' or, 'You can have that'. I'd get something nice for getting good grades, or I'd get it on my own."*

*Ring Revelations*
*Unraveling the Mysteries of Boxing's Past, Present, and Future*

# Table of Contents

Andre Ward..................................................................... 1

The Gypsy King .............................................................. 4

Undefeated ...................................................................... 8

The Heaviest Heavyweight Champion ................................. 10

Boxing Originated in Ancient Greece.................................. 12

The Lightest Heavyweight Champion .................................. 14

Like Jazz ........................................................................ 15

The Punch Numbers.......................................................... 15

Boxing Combinations ....................................................... 18

Everyman ........................................................................ 21

Joe Louis v. Billy Conn .................................................... 21

A Few Essential Boxing Tips for Beginners......................... 23

Most Knockouts and Wins................................................. 26

Fishermen aren't great boxers............................................. 27

Iron Mike ........................................................................ 27

The Importance of Stance, Guard and Footwork in Boxing . 30

"Lights Out"..................................................................... 34

*Ring Revelations*
*Unraveling the Mysteries of Boxing's Past, Present, and Future*

Insomnia.................................................................................. 36

Excellent boxing skills........................................................... 36

Say What?............................................................................... 38

Deontay Wilder "In a league of his own."............................ 39

Most entertaining boxers....................................................... 41

Why MMA Stars Step Into Boxing Rings ........................... 44

Amazing '80s and '90s punchers .......................................... 45

Shadow boxing. ...................................................................... 46

Do Gloves do more harm than bare knuckles? ..................... 46

Sugar Ray Robinson. ............................................................. 47

Old and Young Boxers. ......................................................... 48

Blocking Punches. ................................................................. 51

Julio César Chávez vs. Meldrick Taylor............................... 53

The Resurgence of Boxing..................................................... 55

The Big Four .......................................................................... 58

Hagler v. Hearns -- Anticipation for an Epic Showdown ..... 59

Line up .................................................................................... 60

The Legendary Battle of Jack Dempsey vs. Luis Firpo ........ 61

*Ring Revelations*
*Unraveling the Mysteries of Boxing's Past, Present, and Future*

Boxing helps your mind......................................................... 62

The Title Fight of November 12th, 1982, in Miami .............. 64

Most Consecutive World Title Defenses in Boxing History. 65

Frazier vs. Ali ........................................................................ 66

What's your opinion on the greatest heavyweight ever? ...... 69

Sugar Ray Leonard v. Roberto Duran..................................... 71

The biggest upset .................................................................. 73

More about Health Benefits and Exercise. ........................... 78

The journey of Manny Pacquiao is truly inspirational.......... 81

One for the ages!.................................................................... 82

Walks into a bar .................................................................... 85

Hagler vs. Sugar Ray Leonard............................................... 85

Most Punches Thrown in a Professional Boxing Match....... 86

A Historic Rivalry and Enduring Friendship ....................... 87

Rope-a-Dope ......................................................................... 88

Rumble in the Jungle. ........................................................... 89

Why is boxing called "The Sweet Science?"....................... 90

The longest boxing match...................................................... 93

| | |
|---|---|
| From rags to riches. | 94 |
| The Brown Bomber. | 97 |
| An Interesting fact about George Foreman | 98 |
| The Bite Fight | 100 |
| Quick KOs | 102 |
| Mike Tyson's Near Encounter With a Gorilla | 104 |
| Riddick Bowe v. Andrew Golota -- Strange match | 104 |
| The Evolution and Future of Boxing. | 111 |
| About the author. | 114 |
| We Want to Hear from You! | 115 |

*Ring Revelations*
*Unraveling the Mysteries of Boxing's Past, Present, and Future*

**An Imitation of Life!** *"Boxing is an imitation of life. You get knocked down and you get back up. You don't quit no matter how dark it gets, or whatever adversity passes your way. You just got to keep fighting, coming up the other side and not quitting, no matter what."*

-- **Caleb Plant**, an American professional boxer who held the IBF super middleweight title from 2019 to 2021. He is currently ranked among the top super middleweights in the world.

**Andre Ward** was born in San Francisco, California, the son of Frank Ward, an Irish American, and Madeline Arvie Taylor an African American. Andre's career started when his father took him to a boxing gym in Hayward, California, when he was nine years old.

After his parents fell to drug abuse, Ward was looked after by his godfather, Virgil Hunter, who became his trainer and remained his trainer for the length of his career.

One of the most remarkable achievements in Andre Ward's career was his gold medal win at the 2004 Olympics held in Athens, Greece. This victory catapulted Ward into the international spotlight and laid the foundation for his future success in the professional boxing arena.

Andre Ward's professional boxing career reached its peak when he became the unified light heavyweight champion. Throughout his professional boxing career, Andre Ward remained undefeated, retiring with a perfect record.

One of the defining characteristics of Andre Ward's boxing style was his exceptional defensive skills. His ability to evade punches and counter effectively made him a formidable opponent in the ring.

Andre Ward faced and triumphed over renowned boxers including Sergey Kovalev, Arthur Abraham, and Carl Froch, among others. His victories against these formidable opponents cemented his legacy as one of boxing's elite.

He was named Fighter of the Year by multiple organizations. Andre Ward's exceptional performance inside the ring led to him being recognized as the Fighter of the Year by prestigious organizations such as the *Boxing Writers Association of America* and *The Ring magazine*.

After an illustrious career, Andre Ward officially announced his retirement from professional boxing in September, 2017. His departure marked the end of an era and left a void in the sport. He announced, *"As I walk away from the sport of boxing today, I leave at the top of your glorious mountain, which was always my vision and my dream. I did it. We did it. From the bottom of my heart, thank you to everyone who has played a part in my journey. You know who you are. I could not have done this without you."*

Andre Ward is actively involved in various charitable endeavors, using his platform and influence to make a positive impact on the lives of others. His philanthropic efforts highlight his dedication to giving back to the community.

Andre Ward's illustrious career has earned him a well-deserved place in the Boxing Hall of Fame. Andre Ward's unique boxing style blended power and finesse, making him a force to be reckoned with inside the ring. His ability to deliver devastating punches with precision and grace set him apart from his opponents.

Andre Ward's journey from a young aspiring boxer to a world champion serves as an inspiration to countless individuals pursuing a career in boxing. His sportsmanship, humility, and professionalism have made him a beloved figure in the boxing community.

But it is not just his success in the ring that makes him captivating. Ward's humble demeanor, strong work ethic, and commitment to his family and community set him apart as a role model and inspiration for aspiring athletes. Whether you're a boxing enthusiast or simply someone who appreciates remarkable stories of triumph, Andre Ward's journey will continue to captivate and leave a lasting impact.

*Ring Revelations*
*Unraveling the Mysteries of Boxing's Past, Present, and Future*

*Andre Ward*

**The Gypsy King**. Tyson Fury has taken the boxing world by storm with his feats inside the ring. But beyond his skills in the squared circle, Tyson Fury has a story of resilience, determination and triumph over adversity.

Standing at 6 feet 9 inches tall with lightning quick hands and cat-like reflexes, Tyson Fury possesses the physical gifts to dominate opponents. But it's his fighting style and showmanship that sets him apart from any other boxer on the planet.

Whether he's dancing like a ballerina or taunting foes, Tyson Fury brings the kind of unique excitement that packs arenas and has fans on the edge of their seats!

When he's not dazzling crowds with his ring walks (have you seen his Batman costume entrance?!), Tyson Fury is busy cementing his legacy as one of the best heavyweights of all time.

After battling personal demons and mental health issues, Tyson Fury made an improbable comeback. Rising from the ashes of despair, "The Gypsy King" reclaimed his title as lineal champion in one of the best sports redemption stories ever. It's moments like these that show Tyson Fury's true heart of a champion and inspire millions around the world.

Born on August 12, 1988, in Manchester, England, he hails from a proud Romani family with a strong boxing heritage.

He earned the nickname "The Gypsy King" due to his proud Romani heritage and his dominance in the ring. This nickname reflects his cultural pride and boxing prowess. He said, "I am fighting royalty. I have gypsy kings on both sides of the family."

Fury is a former unified heavyweight champion, achieving boxing's highest honor in 2015 when he defeated Wladimir Klitschko to become the undisputed champion, holding the WBA, IBF, WBO, and IBO titles simultaneously.

With his defeat of Deontay Wilder the first time, Fury became just the second heavyweight in boxing history to hold The Ring Magazine Title twice. He won it the first time when he beat Wladimir Klitschko back in 2015. Floyd Patterson and Muhammad Ali are the only two other boxers to achieve this feat.

He was named after boxing legend Mike Tyson and comes from a family of prizefighters, with his father John Fury also a former professional boxer, exposing him to the sweet science from a young age.

After a period of absence from the ring from 2017 to 2018 due to well-documented personal and mental health issues, Tyson Fury made a sensational comeback in 2018 and 2019, defying expectations in dominant fashion to reclaim his place atop the heavyweight division rankings. This comeback exemplified his resilience and fortitude.

Unlike more stationary heavyweight counterparts, Fury utilizes an unorthodox, elusive fighting style, incorporating swift footwork, angular head movement, and unpredictable punch selection to keep his opponents off-balance. This unique style has brought him success in the ring.

Beyond his skills in the ring, Tyson Fury is also a charismatic and outspoken personality, drawing audiences in with his candid interviews, bold pre-fight statements, and amusing antics.

Known also for his witty verbal jousting with opponents in the buildup to fights, Tyson Fury is a masterful trash-talker, getting inside his foes' heads to help sell tickets and raise excitement.

Open about his personal struggles, Fury has battled depression, addiction, and weight gain, yet emerged stronger through resilience and determination, serving as an inspiration for others facing adversity.

In addition to his boxing career, Tyson Fury is involved in philanthropic efforts, donating sizable funds to mental health advocacy and homeless charities. He utilizes his platform for positive change.

While known primarily for his boxing skills, Fury has also competed in professional wrestling.

Remarkably, Fury remains undefeated in all of his world title fights, underscoring his elite skills, fortitude, and ability to thrive when the stakes are highest under the bright lights.

With his combination of ring mastery, charisma, and international stardom, Tyson Fury has become one of boxing's premier figures, owning a massive, dedicated fanbase that has seen him transcend the sport.

Emotions can win fights. Tyson maintains, "Sometimes emotions can win fights. Sometimes letting your feelings out in a fight can win you the fight. When it means the world to you, it's not just a sports contest - a boxing match for money or belts." So, being yourself is important for boxing success.

*Tyson Fury*

**Undefeated**. Some say the best of the undefeated boxers of all time were Floyd Mayweather Jr., Rocky Marciano, Joe Calzaghe, Edwin Valero, Andre Ward, and Ricardo Lopez, who left their mark on boxing history with their extraordinary skills and never-ending winning streaks. Each fighter brought their own unique style and passion to dominate opponents victory after victory.

**Mayweather** is undoubtedly one of the greatest of all time thanks to his tactical skills, defensive mastery, and his record of 50 wins with no losses! He had 27 knockouts and 12 world championships in five weight classes. His ability to read opponents like a book and strike with laser-like precision made him.

**Marciano** was a total powerhouse who finished his career an unbelievable 49-0 through raw strength, relentless energy, and an iron jaw that could take a punch. With his devastating "Suzie Q" right hand and ability to take a beating, Marciano powered through opponents with his dedication and grit.

**Joe Calzaghe** dominated the super-middleweight division for over a decade while collecting an array of titles on his way to a flawless 46-0 record. Highlights include wins over Chris Eubank, Bernard Hopkins, and Mikkel Kessler - he was just too fast, technical and combo-heavy for anyone to handle!

**Edwin Valero** struck fear into opponents' hearts with his all-knockout record of 27-0 thanks to his aggressive pressure and laser accuracy. He was a true power-puncher who always came forward throwing bombs to end fights early - what explosive talent!

**Andre Ward** kept his undefeated streak alive at 32-0 using his boxing IQ, versatile defense, and technical mastery to outsmart challenges. Ward could adapt his game plan on the fly and control fights with his jab - he was exceptionally smart in the ring!

**Ricardo Lopez** brought a unique blend of offense and defense as the mini-flyweight king with precise power and seemingly endless stamina. His tactical savvy and adaptability made him a nightmare in his division.

These boxers truly left their mark on the sport's history and inspired generations with their unwavering drive and unmatched skill. Their careers set the bar and are studied by all who want to achieve greatness between the ropes. To stay undefeated takes an iron will, top-tier training, tactical planning and the ability to rise to any challenge - that's what made these boxers legends of the game!

## The Heaviest Heavyweight Champion.

There is no limit to how much a boxer may weigh for the heavyweight class.

Nikolai Valuev, a prominent Russian world-class professional boxer and competing in the ring from 1993 through 2009, achieved boxing's highest honor by holding the World Boxing Association (WBA) heavyweight championship on two separate occasions between 2005 and his retirement in 2009.

At an incredible height of 7 feet and peak weight of over 328 pounds, Valuev claimed his place in boxing history by becoming the tallest and heaviest man *ever* to win a world heavyweight title.

Throughout his 16-year boxing career, Valuev consistently leveraged his immense physical attributes to compete against much smaller opponents. In addition to capturing WBA gold twice, he held victories over former titleholders John Ruiz and Evander Holyfield.

While not regarded as the most technically gifted pugilist, Valuev's combination of size, strength and determination allowed him to achieve boxing success.

Since retiring his gloves in 2009, Valuev has transitioned smoothly into politics and now serves as a member of the Russian State Duma. He'll be remembered as a giant in two fields due to his unprecedented stature and accomplishments in both the boxing ring and government.

*Nikolai Valuev*

**Boxing Originated in Ancient Greece.** Boxing has a long and storied history that can be traced back to ancient times. As one of the earliest combat sports, it emerged alongside other Olympic disciplines in Ancient Greece where the foundations of Western athletics were first established.

A primitive form of boxing known as Pygmachia was already a competitive event in the first Olympic Games in 688 BCE. Pygmachia, which roughly translates to "punching with closed fists," bore similarities to modern boxing but also had important differences. Fighters known as pygmaches would engage in boxing matches without gloves and there was no round structure or judges' scoring as seen today.

However, it represented one of the earliest incarnations of the sport of using fists for combat that would evolve greatly over the centuries.

The rules of ancient Greek boxing differed significantly from the modern boxing sport enjoyed today. While boxing remains a physically demanding contest of skill and endurance, the ancient Greek version had regulations that seem foreign to our contemporary understanding of the sport.

Perhaps most notably, there were no defined time limits or separation into rounds. Victories were determined not by judges' scorecards but rather by one opponent either verbally surrendering or becoming physically incapacitated due to injuries sustained in the fight.

Weight classes, a hallmark of modern boxing used to ensure fair and competitive matchups, did not exist in ancient Greece. Competitors of varying sizes were permitted to face off against one another.

Additionally, the battles did not transpire within a regulated space such as a boxing ring. The fights occurred outdoors or in open-air arenas without barriers or boundaries.

The first champion of Olympic boxing was a man named Onomastus of Smyrna at the 28th Olympiad in 688 BC. [1] Onomastus not only emerged victorious in this inaugural competition but also had the distinction of establishing the original set of rules and guidelines for the sport in ancient Greece.

From those early origins grew the sport we now recognize, a testament to its enduring popularity and ability to adapt across eras. The ancient Greeks helped establish boxing as a competitive pastime that would be embraced globally for generations to come.

**Like Chess.** *"In boxing you create a strategy to beat each new opponent, it's just like chess."*

  **-- Lennox Lewis**

**The Lightest Heavyweight Champion.** Bob Fitzsimmons was an unconventional heavyweight champion boxer. Although he had the broad shoulders typically associated with heavyweight fighters, Fitzsimmons' legs more closely resembled those of a welterweight fighter due to their slender physique.

In fact, when Bob made his professional debut, he weighed a mere 148 pounds, making him the lightest boxer ever to claim the heavyweight championship.

During his championship bout against James Corbett, Fitzsimmons faced an uphill battle as Corbett was clearly outboxing him throughout the fight. However, Fitzsimmons was able to land a powerful punch directly to Corbett's solar plexus, effectively ending the fight and claiming the heavyweight title for himself.

In doing so, Fitzsimmons became the first former middleweight champion to ascend to become the heavyweight champion as well.

Decades later, boxer Roy Jones Jr. was able to match this rare feat accomplished by Fitzsimmons. Like Fitzsimmons before him, Jones first captured a middleweight championship but then went on to also become the heavyweight champion, making him only the second boxer in history to hold titles at both the middleweight and heavyweight levels.

Bob Fitzsimmons

**Like Jazz.** *"Boxing is like jazz. The better it is, the less people appreciate it."*

**-- George Foreman**

**The Punch Numbers.** Many boxers and coaches will use a number system to describe the type of punch by giving it a specific number 1 through 6.

1. Jab
2. Cross
3. Lead Hook
4. Rear Hook
5. Lead Uppercut
6. Rear Uppercut

**1. The Jab.** This punch is an important tool in boxing. To perform a proper jab, start with your weight on your rear leg. The amount of weight you can transfer from your rear to your lead leg determines the power of the jab. All punching power comes from the legs. As you throw the jab, push off your rear leg and transfer your weight forward.

Keep your elbow tight to your body and perpendicular to the ground as you throw the punch. Snap the punch by turning your wrist over as you extend your arm. Make contact with your top two knuckles. Once the punch lands, pull your hand straight back toward your face in a defensive guard position. This is called chambering your punches. Bring your hands straight back with your elbows tucked in.

**2. The Cross.** Like the jab, start the cross punch with your weight on your rear leg. The amount of weight transferred from your rear to lead leg again determines power. Focus on pivoting your rear foot to help with weight transfer. As with all punches, power comes from the legs. Throw the cross by pushing off your rear leg and transferring weight forward.

Keep your elbow tight to your body and perpendicular to the ground during the punch. Staying close to your body's midline maximizes power. Snap the punch by turning your wrist over. Rotate your shoulders to add power. Make contact with your top two knuckles. Once landed, chamber the punch by pulling your hand straight back toward your face with elbows tucked in.

**3. Lead Hook Punch**. For the lead hook punch, start with approximately 70% of your weight on your lead foot. As you throw and follow through the punch, shift your weight backward to your rear foot. Pivot your lead foot to maximize weight transfer backward. All power comes from legs and torso rotation. If you can't pick up your lead leg mid-punch, focus on proper weight shift.

Begin the punch one foot outside your body's midline toward your lead side. Keep your hand semi-perpendicular to the ground. Pop your elbow up so it's parallel to the ground. Shift weight back and rotate your torso through the punch. Think of punching around your opponent. Make contact with your top two knuckles and chamber the punch back toward your face.

**4. Rear Hook Punch**. For the rear hook, start with about 70% of your weight on the ball of your rear foot. As you throw the punch, follow through by shifting your weight forward to your lead foot. Pivot your rear foot to maximize weight transfer forward. Power comes from legs and torso rotation.

Begin one foot outside your midline toward your rear side. Keep your hand semi-perpendicular to start. Pop your elbow up parallel to the ground. Shift weight forward and rotate through the punch. Once landed, chamber your hand back into guard position.

**5. Lead Uppercut Punch**. To perform a lead uppercut, start by bending your knees and dropping your center of gravity with most weight on the lead leg. As you throw the punch, explode upward. Power is generated from your lead leg's quadricep.

Keep your hands in guard position to start. Drop your lead hand one foot to waist height. As you explode up, make contact with your arm perpendicular to the floor and palm facing yourself. Hands return immediately to guard. Focus on exploding up and shoulder rotation for power, landing square on your target.

**6. Rear Uppercut Punch**. For a rear uppercut, bend knees and drop into a lower stance with most weight on the rear leg. Explode upward as you throw the punch, with power coming from the rear leg quadricep. Pivot your rear leg to maximize upward momentum.

Keep hands in guard and drop the rear hand one foot to waist height. Make contact with arm perpendicular as you explode up, palm facing yourself. Immediately return hands to guard. Focus on explosion and shoulder rotation to drive power into your target square on the midline.

Continued practice is key to mastering these basic boxing punches. Study the techniques and refer to the number calls during classes to build muscle memory over time. Proper form will allow you to unleash power from your whole body with each strike.

## Boxing Combinations

. Here are just a few effective boxing combinations. Diversifying combinations allow fighters to unleash multiple punches in quick succession, keeping their opponent off balance.

Mastering combinations is an important part of developing boxing skills.

First, most everyone knows the Jab, Cross (1,2) Combination. The 1-2 is one of the first combinations boxers learn as it is simple but effective. Elite fighters in history like Floyd Mayweather and Manny Pacquiao rely on the 1-2. There are different ways to use it, such as using the jab to gauge distance before the cross or to open the opponent's guard for the cross. Beginners should focus on throwing it fast to keep it simple, and can vary the jab speed once proficient.

Next, Jab, Jab, Cross (1,1,2) Combination. This builds on the basic 1-2 by adding a second jab. It prevents opponents from anticipating one jab and keeps pressure on them. It also makes punches harder to time since they don't know if one or two jabs are coming. Beginners should throw it fast initially and then experiment with jab speeds.

Jab, Cross, Left Hook (1,2,3) Combination. One of boxing's most common combinations, it forces opponents to defend all three punches. Keep technique clean on the hook and don't telegraph it. Beginners can start with full speed jab and cross followed by a 50% hook, and practice increasing your hook speed.

The Lead Uppercut, Cross (5,2) Combination. The powerful lead uppercut scores knockouts and backs opponents up. It's effective after landing jabs to drop guards. Beginners focus on clean technique, power from legs, and not telegraphing intent while keeping chins down.

Next, the Jab, Right Hook (1,4) Combination. This scores knockouts. Rotate hips on the hook to transfer power. Beginners throw full speed jab and hook, practicing hip rotation and keeping chins down and backs straight.

Next, the Cross, Left Hook, Cross (2,3,2) Combination. This is a difficult to block combo from varying angles. Rotate hips fully on last two punches. Vary speeds to make it harder to deflect and be ready to counter counters.

Also try the Right Uppercut, Left Hook (6,3) Combination. Set this power combo up by forcing lowered guards with previous jabs. Bend knees on the uppercut and rotate torso on the hook.

The Jab, Cross, Lead Uppercut (1,2,5) Combination. This adds a powerful lead uppercut to the basic 1-2. Vary speeds to keep opponents guessing and throw combinations fast.

Left Uppercut, Right Uppercut, Left Hook (5, 6, 3). This combination is effective when an opponent is pinned against the ropes. Throwing hard left and right uppercuts first forces the opponent to lower their guard, exposing them to a left hook. Depending on an opponent's guard, a left hook to the body in this scenario can be just as impactful as one to the head.

Jab, Cross, Jab (1, 2, 1). This outside range combination scores points and can stun opponents. Mixing it with combinations like double jab and jab, jab, cross keeps opponents guessing.

Jab, Right Uppercut, Left Hook (1, 6, 3). This uses the right uppercut but requires close range. Feints and footwork can be used to get inside or throw punches to lower the guard before moving in. From close range, the jab is followed by the right uppercut, dropping the guard for the left hook.

Right Cross, Left Hook, Right Uppercut (2, 3, 6). Similar to 5, 6, 3 but substituting a cross for the first uppercut. The cross stuns and the left hook exploits the opening, with the right uppercut further dropping the guard.

With practice, boxers can learn to execute combinations incorporating speed, power and accuracy to gain advantages in matches. Creativity in developing new combinations is also encouraged. Mastering combinations is key to winning fights and scoring knockouts.

**Everyman**. "Every man's got to figure to get beat sometime. Once that bell rings you're on your own. It's just you and the other guy."

**-- Joe Louis**

**Joe Louis v. Billy Conn**. On June 18, 1941, Joe Louis defended his heavyweight title against Billy Conn in a highly anticipated bout held at Yankee Stadium in New York City. Joe Louis, known as the "Brown Bomber," was making the 18th defense of his championship.

However, Conn was no ordinary challenger. The "Pittsburgh Kid" had previously held the light heavyweight title and dropped weight classes in hopes of dethroning the division's elite competitors.

At weigh-in, Louis tipped the scales at 199.5 pounds, a full 25 pounds heavier than Conn who was at a trim 174-pound weight. Despite the size disparity, Conn utilized his speed and technical boxing skills, outboxing Louis through the early rounds.

In the tenth, Conn reportedly told Louis within a clinch "You've got yourself a fight tonight." Both fighters recognized the competitiveness of the bout.

Entering the championship rounds, the crowd was fully engaged as the action intensified. In the twelfth, Conn landed a powerful left hook that nearly felled the defending champion.

At the final bell, Conn expressed confidence in his ability to knock out Louis. However, when Conn closed the distance in pursuit of the knockout, Louis countered with fury, connecting with a decisive right hand that flattened Conn.

Though they engaged in a legendary contest, Louis and Conn developed a lifelong friendship in its aftermath. Conn would often jokingly ask Louis "Couldn't you have let me hold the title for just six months?" to which Louis would reply, "You had it for twelve rounds - that wasn't long enough for you to keep it!"

Their June 1941 bout has been cemented as an iconic heavyweight title fight between two boxing greats.

*Joe Louis, "The Brown Bomber"*

## A Few Essential Boxing Tips for Beginners.

Here are basic boxing points that make a difference and put you a step ahead of most others if you don't already know these tips.

**Diversify Your Punch Combinations.** There are many punch combinations that can be effective in boxing as pointed out in the previous section (Boxing Combinations). Some basic combinations include the 1-2 punch and hook-straight punch. More advanced boxers utilize a variety of combinations. The key to having a strong offense is mixing up your combinations to keep your opponent guessing.

It is important to vary your punch output to have a great offense. Practice different combinations using focus mitts to refine your technique while also building power with heavy bag work. Once comfortable, apply these techniques in sparring sessions. Sparring allows you to experience the real flow of a fight.

Be sure not to rely on the same combinations each time as your opponent will start to anticipate your offense. Instead, switch between targeting the head and body to keep them from predicting where your punches will land. Moving between upper and lower punches makes it harder for opponents to anticipate your offense.

**Good Head Movement.** Be unpredictable. Not only does good head movement improve defense, but it also adds unpredictability to combinations. Bobbing and weaving from side to side while punching makes you a harder target to hit while seamlessly transferring your weight and momentum.

Constant head movement is a mark of a skilled boxer. It takes focus to incorporate head movement especially for novice boxers who must also focus on ring skills. But practicing head movement means focusing on perfecting all aspects of technique. Head movement also makes you less likely to get hit with clean shots since it adds unpredictability on offense and defense. Shadow box in front of a mirror to refine your head movement.

**Know Proper Positioning for Combinations.** Learning when to throw combinations is key to accuracy. Novices often initiate punches from too far away, leaving them open after overextending. Improved footwork leads to better positioning within optimal range. It's also important to exit combinations at angles rather than moving straight back which is easier to counter.

**Keep away from your opponent's power hand.** As a general rule, circle away from your opponent's power hand so their hardest punches have less impact. Good positioning through footwork allows you to unleash combinations while dancing around opponents.

**Rest is essential for having a productive training session.** Sleep allows the body and mind to reset after a long day. Lack of sleep leaves you feeling drained while adequate rest ensures sharpness and focus needed for boxing's demands. Conditioning plays a vital role in boxing and improving conditioning overall makes you a better boxer able to push physical limits.

**Maintain eye contact** with your opponent at all times to better anticipate their attacks and protect yourself from counterattacks. Locking eyes allows you to stay one step ahead and react appropriately in any situation.

**Foot placement**. There is a constant battle for foot placement when you're boxing. Wherever possible, keep your lead foot on the outside of your opponent's lead foot, especially when attacking. This outside position allows you to effectively unleash offenses.

**Stance**. When facing taller opponents, a lower stance can help minimize the impact of their punches by lowering your profile. However, be careful not to maintain a low stance for too long as it can quickly deplete your stamina. Build leg strength through exercises like squats and calf raises.

**Sidestepping** is an underutilized technique that can be effective on both offense and defense. A quick sidestep can circle you away from power shots and exposes openings when you move laterally.

**Clinches.** Learning to clinch provides an opportunity to take a break in close quarters. It can also frustrate opponents when used frequently, draining their energy. Develop smooth clinching skills through sparring practice.

**Conserve energy** by only throwing purposeful punches and looking for openings rather than constant volume. Pace yourself to avoid tiring too quickly. Advanced techniques like feints create opportunities without expending much energy.

**Defense** should not be forgotten -- the goal is to land combinations while sustaining minimal damage. Absorbing punches depletes stamina and slows you over time. Always protect yourself as much as possible.

## Most Knockouts and Wins

Knockouts are the most iconic way a boxing match ends, where one of the boxers is dropped to the ground without being able to stand after 10 seconds of countdown. But do you know the professional boxer who knocked out the most opponents?

That answer is the British Billy Bird, with 138 knockouts as part of his impressive 260 wins during his 28-year-long career. Billy was a taxi driver when he wasn't boxing. [2] Archie Moore is second with 132 KOs. [3]

Another British man Len Wickwar holds the record for the most boxing matches. He fought in 473 bouts and simultaneously holds the most wins under his belt of 342. [4] He fought more verified professional fights than any other boxer in history and those 473 matches had a total of 4,020 rounds fought in his 19-year career. [5]

**Fishermen aren't great boxers.** *Why are fishermen bad at boxing?*

*A. Because they only throw hooks.*

**Iron Mike.** Mike Tyson is considered one of the greatest professional boxers of all time. Nicknamed "Iron Mike" and "Kid Dynamite" early in his career, Tyson was later known as "The Baddest Man on the Planet."

Tyson came out like a star winning his first 19 professional fights by knockout, with 12 occurring in the first round. At just 20 years, 4 months, and 22 days old, Tyson became the youngest boxer ever to win a heavyweight title. [6] He was the first heavyweight to simultaneously hold the WBA, WBC, and IBF titles.

Tyson further solidified his status by becoming the lineal champion when he defeated Michael Spinks in just 91 seconds of the first round in 1988.

But in 1990, Tyson suffered one of the biggest upsets in boxing history when he was knocked out by underdog Buster Douglas.

Then the downward trend continued. In 1992, Tyson was convicted of rape and sentenced to six years in prison, though he was released on parole after three years.

After his release in 1995, Tyson embarked on a series of comeback fights. He regained the WBA and WBC titles in 1996, joining an elite group of boxers at that time (Floyd Patterson, Muhammad Ali, Tim Witherspoon, Evander Holyfield and George Foreman) who had regained the heavyweight championship after losing it.

Over the course of his career, Tyson established himself as one of the most celebrated and skilled heavyweight champions of all time. His knockout power and dominance in the ring earned him widespread recognition as "The Baddest Man on the Planet" during his prime.

But in 1997, the clash between Tyson and Holyfield has taken on a lore all its own, and it was dubbed "The Sound and the Fury". It will forever live in infamy as "The Bite Fight". Over time we still speculate on the events of that night.

When the third round began, nobody could have foreseen the savagery to unfold. In a moment of unbridled rage, Tyson lunged at Holyfield sinking his teeth into his opponent's cartilage. He tore away a chunk, spitting it in disgust upon the canvas below. A maddened Tyson then tossed the agonized Holyfield around the ring as the blood flowed free. It was mayhem unleashed.

Though deducted two points solely, the commission permitted Tyson to fight on. But Mike was not sated, going after Holyfield's other ear and leaving the officials no choice but expulsion. Pandemonium reigned as Tyson battled all in pursuit of Holyfield once more.

Some say Tyson bit Holyfield's eat for retaliation for Holyfield's head blows, which brutalized rather than buffered. Others say Tyson probably knew his end was near and sought escape from the beating.

The truths buried in Tyson's mind that eve are shrouded in complexity, and perhaps going back to his days in the penitentiary years prior. One thing is irrefutable - we may never witness such a shocking and unforgettable bout as "The Bite Fight". It endures as one of the most bizarre and unbelievable moments in athletic history.

Nevertheless, Mike is still at it! At the time of this writing, 58-year-old Mike has a bout scheduled with heavyweight 27-year-old Jake Paul on the 20$^{th}$ day of July 2024 at AT&T Stadium, home of the Dallas Cowboys, in Arlington, Texas. Expect the unexpected when it comes to Mike!

*Mike Tyson*

*"Everyone has a plan until they get punched in the face."*

-- **Mike Tyson.**

# The Importance of Stance, Guard and Footwork in Boxing.

Having a proper boxing stance is crucial, as it forms the basis for both offense and defense.

In your stance, place your lead foot slightly forward, angling your rear foot at approximately 45 degrees. Distribute your weight evenly on both feet with knees bent slightly. This balanced positioning allows you to easily change levels.

Your guard is key to protection. Hold both gloves at head level, with your lead glove forward to parry or deflect jabs. Position your rear glove closer to your chin or cheek to block hooks or crosses. This shields your head from primary strikes in boxing.

Footwork also plays a pivotal defensive role. Stay light on your toes for agility and quickness to exit an opponent's range. Laterally move side to side rather than straight back, making you a more elusive target. If your opponent lunges, pivot on your lead foot to change your angle and cause their punch to miss.

There are different guards. First, the traditional boxing guard stance. Hands are high protecting the chin while allowing for blocking of hooks and punches. The elbows are low enough to block body shots too.

This stance offers flexibility for head movement. Hands too high makes bobbing and weaving difficult, while hands too low makes blocking take longer. Notable boxers like Anthony Joshua and Gennady Golovkin utilize this textbook style. However, its frequent use makes it easier to exploit.

**Philly Shell Guard**. Originally called the "crab shell," the Philly shell offers great protection when used correctly. The lead hand stays low to block body shots while the rear hand stays high to catch jabs and hooks. Furthermore, the low lead hand makes incoming jabs harder to see.

Floyd Mayweather famously employed this difficult to master style. He even took hits learning it but perfected shoulder rolling to deflect crosses and create openings for his own attacks. This Philly Shell Guard is riskier against an opponent in the opposite stance due to exposed hooks and crosses.

**High Guard.** Notably used by Ronald "Winky" Wright, Canelo Alvarez, and Vasyl Lomachenko, the high guard keeps the hands in prime position to parry straight shots. The parry-cross combination is especially effective against opposite-stance jabs.

Elbows must stay tucked to defend against uppercuts. High guards invite body shots, so conditioning is important. Jab distance and vision is also reduced, signaling the boxer may be hurt and stalling. Pressure fighters can maintain distance and target the body against this guard.

**Peekaboo Boxing Guard.** Developed by Cus D'Amato for Mike Tyson, the peekaboo is ideal for stocky pressure fighters. With an emphasis on head movement and forward momentum, it poses problems for taller foes.

Toes point forward for better lateral movement without losing balance. Hands cover the cheeks and body to simultaneously protect chin and core. However, reliance on timing and reflexes makes this guard predictable and limited over the long-term.

**Cross-Guard**. Rarely seen but used to great effect by Archie Moore, Ken Norton, and George Foreman, the cross-guard forms arms across the torso. It protects well but hampers powerful punches. Exposed ribs make liver shots a concern. Nonetheless, it presents an intriguing style after practice.

Ultimately, no single guard is completely right or wrong. Experimentation is key to finding one's best risk-reward approach within the ring.

Footwork also plays a pivotal defensive role. Stay light on your toes for agility and quickness to exit an opponent's range. Laterally move side to side rather than straight back, making you a more elusive target. If your opponent lunges, pivot on your lead foot to change your angle and cause their punch to miss.

Proper stance, guard, and footwork form the solid foundation for blocking techniques in boxing. Mastering these fundamentals lays the groundwork for both offense and defense in the ring.

**Perfect.** *"God only made one thing in this world that's perfect - and that's my boxing record."*

-- **Floyd Mayweather, Jr.** Record 50 wins no losses. [7]

*Floyd Mayweather, Jr.*

**"Lights Out"** Former three-division American boxing champion James "Lights Out" Toney always considered himself a natural-born talent, having possessed a distinct ability to fight from an early age. By the time he first stepped into a boxing gym as a teenager, Toney knew he was made to be a boxer.

With a unique flow to both his offense and defense, Toney utilized incredible head movement and footwork coupled with astonishing reflexes to stifle opponents with his technical mastery. Toney would often toy with opponents, allowing them to tee off their hardest shots only to find nothing but air.

Toney loved to stay in the pocket, hiding in corners and hanging out along the ropes — all areas of the ring most fighters were uncomfortable to be in. He excelled in the most dangerous of circumstances and always came out on top.

In 1991 and 2003, Toney was voted Fighter of the Year by The Ring magazine and the Boxing Writers Association of America. He is one of the greatest middleweight fighters of all time.

*James "Lights out" Toney*

**Demonstrating Skill.** *"There is a strategic and technical aspect to boxing, as there are established rules and techniques.*

*"However, since the beginning, humans have been drawn to witnessing combat. By engaging in combat, one displays the capabilities and vulnerabilities of the human body. The goal is not self-sacrifice for spectators' entertainment, but to*

*demonstrate one's skill in defeating an opponent honorably through strictly bodily means.*

*"It is not a thirst for blood, but rather an appreciation of what the human form can endure and achieve through combat as an artistic performance."*

-- **Ghaleya Aldhafiri**, Author of "Spaces in Culture."

**Insomnia.** A boxer was having trouble sleeping. So, he went to see a doctor. The doctor asks "Have you tried counting sheep?"

The boxer replied, "I have but every time I get to the count of eight, I stand up."

**Excellent boxing skills.** Here are a few well-known fighters who most say have the greatest ring skills in professional boxing. What do you think?

**Sugar Ray Robinson.** This sensational welterweight and middleweight dominated from 1940 to 1965, amassing a record of 175-19-6-2 with 109 knockouts. Robinson utilized movement, speed, and intelligence to outmaneuver foes, keeping them off balance with his jab while delivering hurtful power shots. His instincts and talents were truly remarkable.

Even Roger Mayweather believes Robinson was a superior technician to his nephew Floyd.

**Manny Pacquiao.** He competed in professional boxing from 1995 to 2021. Considered by boxing historians as one of the greatest professional boxers of all time, Pacquiao is the only boxer in history to win twelve major world titles across eight different weight divisions.

Manny is also the first boxer in history to win the linear championship in five different weight divisions. Additionally, Pacquiao was the first boxer in history to win major world titles in four of the original eight weight divisions of boxing, commonly referred to as the "glamor divisions": flyweight, featherweight, lightweight and welterweight.

**Muhammad Ali.** While other heavyweights like Joe Louis had more punching pop, Ali exhibited the finest technical boxing of any in his weight class. He dazzled with incredible hand speed, footwork, and mastery of defensive maneuvers like the "Ali Shuffle." This incredible quickness allowed him to outclass most opponents.

**Joe Louis.** Arguably the best heavyweight ever, Louis' 68-3 record and thunderous power are legendary. However, he also exhibited fine technical skills, throwing punches with accuracy, speed and balance despite lacking elite footwork.

**Floyd Mayweather Jr.** His 50-0 perfect mark and mastery of all punches brands Mayweather among the greats. He combines athleticism with power and showmanship, possessing the ability to hurt foes while also outboxing them with speed and movement.

**Sugar Ray Leonard.** A 1976 Olympic champion, Leonard used hand speed, ring generalship, and surprising power to defeat stronger foes like Roberto Duran, Thomas Hearns, and Marvin Hagler over his 36-3-1 career spanning five weight classes. He showed fine defensive skills while possessing a formidable chin.

*Sugar Ray Leonard*

**Say What?** *"I've seen George Foreman shadow boxing, and the shadow won."*

**-- Muhammad Ali**

## Deontay Wilder "In a league of his own."

Deontay Wilder is an American pro boxer who has fought professionally since 2008.

He had an outstanding record of 41 wins and he has established himself as one of the most dominant heavyweight boxers in the world today. Tyson Fury was the first boxer to beat Deontay and he was also recently beaten by Joseph Parker and will most likely have a rematch with parker in 2024.

Wilder was known for his incredible knockout power, having stopped 40 of his 41 opponents via KO for an astonishing KO rate of 98%. An even more impressive stat is that 30 of those KOs came inside of the first three rounds of the bout. Wilder has notable knockout victories over fighters such as Chris Arreola, Dominic Breazeale, Luis Ortiz, Malik Scott, and Bermane Stiverne.

One remarkable aspect of Wilder's punching prowess is his physical stature. Standing at a height of 6 feet 7 inches, Wilder is certainly tall for a heavyweight but is relatively lean, typically weighing in around 220 pounds. Despite his slight frame, Wilder possesses truly devastating power in both hands. His shocking one-punch knockout of Dominic Breazeale in May 2019 left no question about Wilder's ability to end a fight with a single blow.

Malik Scott, who was knocked out by Wilder in just 96 seconds, commented that unusual speed contributes greatly to

Wilder's knockout ability. "Who gets there faster with the power is Deontay out of anybody I ever been in with."

Retired heavyweight boxer Richard Towers, who has reportedly sparred many top heavyweights including Anthony Joshua, Wladimir and Vitali Klitschko, Tyson Fury, and Wilder himself had high praise for Wilder's punching prowess. Towers recently told The Sun, "I've sparred with every heavyweight you could think of, except Joseph Parker. And I know when it comes to power, Deontay Wilder was in a league of his own."

*Deontay Wilder*

**The brighter side of being hit**. *"My father taught me, in boxing, that when you - particularly when you get hit in the face for the first time - you're going to panic.*

*"But instead of panicking, just accept it. Stay calm. And any time anybody hits you, they always leave themselves open to be hit."*

    **-- Rudy Giuliani**

**Most entertaining boxers.** Certain boxers attract fans not only through their in-ring skills but also through their compelling personalities. Those who possess the ability to effectively communicate often secure higher compensation by generating excitement around their bouts. Muhammed Ali stands out as one of the most charismatic boxers, laying the groundwork for strategically promoting a fight.

While some fighters stir discussion with their remarks outside of competition, it adds interest to the combat sport. The most marketable fighters may find themselves polarizing, motivating some fans into avid detractors who are willing to pay to witness their potential defeat. Whether through charm, confidence, or humor, these boxers effortlessly captured attention from their audience.

**Tyson Fury** effectively demonstrates skills in communication, and his personality matches the magnitude of his physical stature. Whether making a grand entrance to a press event adorned in a Batman suit or making an entrance to a fight seated on a throne, Fury has mastered attracting attention from the boxing community and captivating spectators.

**Ricardo Mayorga** is known for relentless remarks in promotion leading up to most of his fights, coupled with notable habits outside of competition. The former two-weight world champion deserves recognition for enticing Oscar De La Hoya out of retirement through provocative rhetoric, contributing to one of the most stimulating pre-fight build-ups in boxing history.

**Héctor Camacho** resembled a more skilled and athletic version of Mayorga. With a propensity for bold statements, he consistently delivered in competition. Known for his vibrant personality, Camacho attracted attention at the peak of his career.

His entrances added entertainment value themselves, featuring unique styles and eye-catching costumes that added to allure as a must-watch figure in the boxing world.

**Adrien Broner** stands out as one of the rare boxers to achieve multiple world championships across four weight classes, but successes in competition are not the only factors contributing to widespread popularity. Skillful comedy and showmanship have significantly contributed to appeal.

**Floyd Mayweather** stands as one of the most financially successful pay-per-view attractions in the history of sports, achieving high revenue notwithstanding relatively low knockout ratios in prominent fights. Ability to craft a compelling public image played a pivotal role in accomplishments.

Mayweather is an image of confidence and flamboyance, creating magnetic intrigue enticing boxing audiences to pay to witness in action, with many hoping to see face defeat. Throughout career, Floyd accumulated around 24 million pay-per-view purchases, contributing to total revenue of $1.67 billion.

**Prince Naseem Hamed** is often regarded as one of most influential British fighters of last century. Unique combination of flair, skill, and unwavering confidence established one of most captivating public figures in history of boxing. Hamed's impact has drawn comparisons to legendary Muhammad Ali, not only for prowess as fighter, but also for prowess as performer and entertainer in competition. Influence extends beyond era, serving as inspiration for some of boxing's contemporary greats.

**Muhammed Ali's** fame transcended not only extraordinary talent but also provocative and outlandish public image. The heavyweight champion is credited with initiating trend of boxers becoming own promoters, using creative rhyme schemes and spoken-word poetry in press events, interviews, and throughout entertainment career.

Undoubtedly, Ali stands as one of the most influential, charismatic, and recognized boxers of all time, leaving indelible mark on sport and popular culture as whole.

## Why MMA Stars Step Into Boxing Rings. Some
MMA fighters transitioned to boxing but the top boxers seem to avoid competitions in the MMA octagon.

Conor McGregor was the first MMA fighter to crossover into professional boxing. Since then, other fighters such as Ben Askren, Tyron Woodley, Nate Diaz, and Francis Ngannou have competed in boxing matches. On the other hand, few top boxers have entered the MMA arena at this time in history.

There may be several factors that help explain this divergence. First, boxing remains the more lucrative sport, with main event participants in boxing pay-per-view events typically earning higher purses than their MMA counterparts. Francis Ngannou secured a guaranteed $8 million purse against Tyson Fury, exceeding his entire prior MMA career earnings of less than $4 million.

Additionally, competing in MMA requires mastery of multiple disciplines such as wrestling, grappling, kicking, boxing, and more over lengthy training periods. Transitioning boxers would need significant time to develop grappling proficiency, risking their reputations and legacy in their primary sport.

Conversely, MMA athletes already receive boxing training as part of their regular regimen. This transition therefore seems to involve less training.

Finally, MMA seems to inherently carry a higher injury risk due to factors like smaller gloves and increased vulnerability to leg or choke attacks.

For boxers near retirement, a lucrative yet comparatively safer boxing match is understandable. But who knows what the future will hold?

## Amazing '80s and '90s punchers.
Tyrell Biggs established himself as a formidable heavyweight contender in the 1980s, competing against some of the division's fiercest competitors. Here are what Tyrell reportedly viewed when he faced some of the toughest in the '80s -- '90s.

A 1984 Olympic gold medalist, Biggs turned professional that same year and quickly worked his way up the ranks. Within just three years, he had earned a title shot against the reigning undisputed heavyweight champion, "Iron" Mike Tyson. Their July 1987 bout represented the biggest fight of Biggs' career, though he ultimately fell to Tyson via seventh round stoppage.

Biggs went on to face another legendary heavyweight in Lennox Lewis in 1990, this time being defeated even more convincingly via third round knockout. While both Tyson and Lewis handed Biggs crushing losses, he named a relatively unknown fighter, Jeff Sims, as the strongest and hardest-hitting opponent he ever faced. Their 1986 bout saw Sims break Biggs' collarbone with a powerful shot, demonstrating just how formidable a puncher he was.

When reflecting on these heavyweight giants decades later, Biggs maintained that Sims possessed a level of raw strength and punching power that even Tyson and Lewis could not match. However, he acknowledged Tyson's continual improvement as a professional, stating that the version of "Iron Mike" he faced in 1987 would have defeated any fighter from any era on that particular night due to his overwhelming form.

While Sims packed the most devastating power, Biggs recognized Tyson's all-around skill set and peak conditioning as what made him the best opponent he ever stepped into the ring with.

**Shadow boxing.** "I asked my trainer at the gym if I could start shadow boxing."

He replied, "Knock yourself out!"

## Do Gloves do more harm than bare knuckles?

Some say boxing gloves do more substantial injury.

Contrary to common belief, boxing gloves may cause more harm to an opponent than punching with bare hands.

The human hand is surprisingly fragile, as evidenced by bare-knuckle boxing where punches are thrown less frequently due to this vulnerability. Without protective gloves, athletes understandably limit full-force punches to avoid injury.

However, boxing gloves provide cushioning, allowing punches to be thrown harder and more often without hesitation. While external injuries are less likely, repeated forceful punches can lead to internal issues such as concussions and long-term brain damage.

Additionally, gloves add weight to punches, increasing their kinetic energy. Therefore, while boxing gloves shield hands, they may ironically result in more serious injuries to an opponent.

**Sugar Ray Robinson.** Sugar Ray Robinson is considered one of the greatest boxers in history. However, prior to one bout, Robinson dreamed of fatally injuring his opponent in the ring. As a result, he initially wanted to cancel the fight. His minister convinced him to proceed after discussing the dream. [8]

Robinson fought and knocked out his opponent, Jimmy Doyle, in the eighth round. Doyle was helped from the canvas but later died in the hospital that same day.

Doyle had intended to use his earnings to purchase a home for his mother. Upon learning this, Robinson donated the money he earned from his next four bouts to buy the house for Doyle's mother.

While a tragic event, Robinson's actions demonstrated his character and commitment to honoring his fallen opponent even in the aftermath of the fight.

*Sugar Ray Robinson*

**Old and Young Boxers.** The oldest professional boxer was British fighter Steve Ward, who had his first professional bout at the impressive age of 64 years old in 1976. [9]

For the oldest world title holder, that distinction belongs to Bernard Hopkins who was one of the most successful boxers over the past three decades. He won a world title (WBC International light heavyweight title) at 49 years old! [10]

Another notable achievement was by heavyweight champion George Foreman. Foreman captured a heavyweight title at 46 years old, making him the oldest heavyweight champion in history.

Today, Foreman is still regarded as a legend in the sport due to his dominance in the 1960s. He also holds the distinction of being the second oldest boxer to ever win a world title.

Patrick Clifford Daley, also known as Nipper Pat Daly, was a British boxer who competed professionally from 1923 to 1931. He made his professional debut at a young age, around 9 or 10 years old. [11]

In his mid-teens, Daly achieved widespread fame in British boxing as the "Wonderboy". He retired from professional boxing at the age of 17.

Renowned sportswriter Frank Butler praised Daly as "the best young prospect we ever had." He is likely the youngest boxer to ever be ranked in the top ten of The Ring magazine's world ratings. It is believed that Daly was also the youngest ever professional boxer.

"Nipper" Pat Daly had his busiest year in 1929 with 33 total fights, winning 29, losing 3 by stoppage, and drawing 1. Among his victories were wins over champions from Belgium, Britain, Germany, and former Olympians. At just 16 years old, The Ring magazine ranked Daly #10 in the world at bantamweight. An offer was made for Daly to fight in the US, but his manager refused.

In 1930, Daly moved to lightweight but suffered concussions in losses to future champions. He tried to continue but opponents were below his previous level. At just 17, he realized he would not be a world champion and retired.

Daly was known for his fast jab, footwork, skills, and ring intelligence. After retiring, he stayed involved in boxing as a trainer. [12]

Well-known actor Liam Neeson is widely recognized as a highly accomplished film star and actor having achieved significant commercial success and critical acclaim in his career spanning decades. Liam has portrayed memorable characters across multiple blockbuster franchises securing his status among Hollywood's most bankable stars.

However, what some may find interesting is that Neeson's involvement in boxing dates back long before embarking on his storied film career. He began boxing at the young age of nine years old at his local club in Northern Ireland, a pursuit he remained dedicated to for over eight years until he reached seventeen.

As it turns out, Neeson demonstrated clear natural talent and skill in the sport, winning multiple regional titles as an amateur boxer during the span of his involvement.

Perhaps this early background and proficiency in boxing partly explains Neeson's convincing and commanding presence within the action and martial arts genres as he has become so synonymous with on the big screen.

*Liam Neeson*

**Blocking Punches.** At its core, boxing involves participants aiming to land more punches than their opponents in hopes of securing a knockout blow or winning the bout via decision. While casual observers may view boxing as focusing on offense, a deeper understanding reveals defense is equally or more important.

The 2023 super-fight between Gervonta Davis and Ryan Garcia highlighted this. Garcia out-landed Davis in early rounds but

Davis took advantage of defensive holes to win via seventh round knockout, after dropping Garcia in round two. Davis studied under Floyd Mayweather, who dominated boxing for over 23 years relying on defense late in his career.

Blocking is fundamental to good defense since boxers cannot evade every attack. Ideally you evade punches, but predicting opponents isn't always possible. The next best thing is to block attacks and minimize damage. Successful blocks also prevent opponent points and open counterattack opportunities.

There are four main blocking techniques:

1. **High Block** - Slide gloves up to rest knuckles on face at eyebrow level, effectively blocking straight face shots. Bring gloves higher to sides of head, absorbing impact but exposing body.

2. **Low Block** - Like high blocks but lower to protect torso. Lead side involves lowering stance while keeping lead hand around hip height. Rear side keeps rear hand at shoulder height while rotating, though this exposes head.

3. **Catching** - Deflect straight punches by forcefully pushing opponent's hand back into their face, like catching a baseball. Keep head behind hand in case catch is incomplete.

4. **Parrying** - Deflect straight attacks to open counters. Knock punches off course right before impact from outside range. When done correctly, leaves opponent exposed to counterattacks. Lead side involves slapping punches down.

Rear side involves hitting punches down while keeping elbow high.

## Julio César Chávez vs. Meldrick Taylor.

The boxing world had eagerly awaited the super fight between undefeated Mexican champion Julio César Chávez and the rising American star Meldrick Taylor.

With an astounding record of 68 wins and no losses, Chávez was considered the toughest pound-for-pound fighter in the sport.

However, Taylor had quickly ascended the rankings with his lightning-fast combinations and dynamic boxing skills, earning the nickname of "the next Sugar Ray Leonard." All eyes were on this highly touted matchup to see which warrior would emerge victorious.

From the opening bell, the sold-out arena was engulfed in pulsating energy as the two gladiators went to war inside the ring. True to his billing, Taylor came out swinging with impressive flurries.

But the iron-chinned Chávez refused to back down, taking Taylor's best shots and continuing to stalk his opponent relentlessly. Though Taylor landed the higher volume, Chávez found his mark with well-timed counterpunches.

As the championship rounds progressed, the damage from the sustained battle began to take a toll on both combatants.

Taylor's face was a swollen and bloody mess, while Chávez showed signs of wear from Taylor's early onslaught.

Coming into the final round, Taylor was clearly worn down but still battling courageously. Then, in a controversial conclusion, Chávez dropped Taylor with a knockdown and the referee jumped in with just two seconds left on the clock to stop the contest—awarding Chávez the victory.

The epic 12-round war between these legends had ended in a conclusion that would be debated for years. While both fighters cemented their place among the sport's immortals with their gritty performances, they also left the boxing world buzzing about one of the all-time classic matchups.

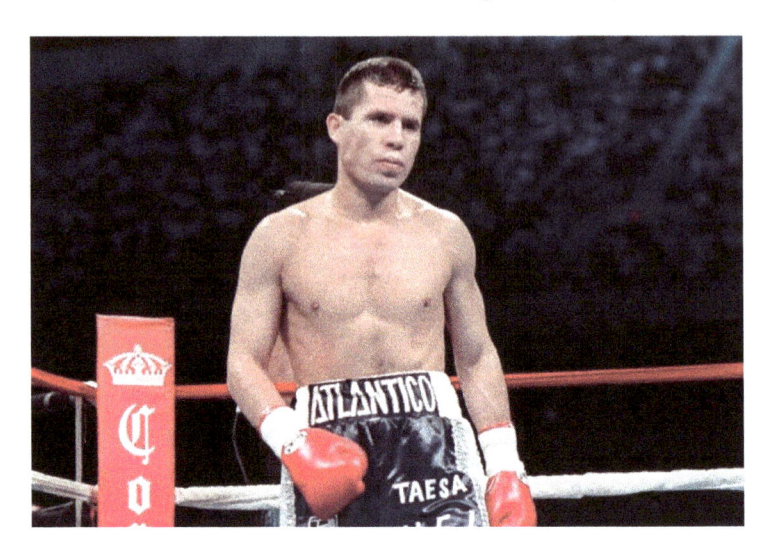

*Julio César Chávez*

**The Resurgence of Boxing.** Exactly five years ago, HBO withdrew from the boxing promotion business in a move that shocked the sport. "I had heard about it before I read about it," recalled Seth Abraham, the former head of HBO Sports, on the network's departure. Abraham was president of Madison Square Garden at the time. "It was very disappointing to see that brand exit the space."

HBO's withdrawal had a significant impact, taking with it memories of great boxing matches. Showtime Sports, HBO's long-time rival in broadcasting boxing, also exited the sport somewhat recently. Showtime's final boxing broadcast was on December 16th, 2022, featuring a super middleweight title fight. Their last pay-per-view event was on November 25th for an interim super middleweight championship.

Where boxing was once a major draw for sports fans, attracting large audiences just 50 years ago, its popularity seems to be waning. Younger audiences seem to favor mixed martial arts and entertainment like WWE. There seems to be a decline of print media depriving boxing a bit of critical coverage and storytelling.

While the sport still sees the occasional high-profile matchup, its long-term commercial viability remains a bit in question without reforms to modernize its business operations and fan experience.

But there appears to be a resurgence. The sport of boxing struggled over the past couple of decades and has made a resurgence recently thanks to captivating personalities, thrilling matchups, and innovative marketing strategies adopted from newer combat sports like mixed martial arts.

Heavy investments in boxing have enabled some of the biggest matchups fans requested while celebrity boxing continues attracting younger fans. Boxing now repurposes its product for different audiences.

Boxing needs heroes and storylines engaging fans. It suffered losing Floyd Mayweather and Manny Pacquiao, the top names since the late 1990s.

While talent remains ample, boxers with charisma filling arenas aren't easy to find. Thankfully, Terence Crawford, Gervonta Davis, and Naoya Inoue now play that role alongside stars Claressa Shields, Katie Taylor and Amanda Serrano.

Boxing improved getting best fighters against each other versus a decade ago. Even Mayweather-Pacquiao took over a decade organizing, both past primes when agreed. It seems fans wanted younger versions, potentially creating a historic rivalry.

New stars understand such scenarios. Gervonta Davis v. Ryan Garcia generated over 1.2 million pay-per-view buys for $84.99 showing fans spending on desired fights. The event also generated approximately $22.8 million in ticket sales revenue, with additional revenue earned from sponsorships and advertising. [13]

Being a fan has been rewarding seeing Tyson Fury-Deontay Wilder, Terence Crawford-Errol Spence, and Tyson Fury-Francis Ngannou.

Boxing capitalized on streaming's rising popularity globally delivering events anywhere via internet.

Hardcore fans initially disliked celebrity boxing but its impact remains undeniable. KSI and Jake Paul took things to new levels hosting sold out arenas. Tyson v. Jake Paul will most likely get massive attention.

Promoters now work closely with online influencers reaching new audiences. Spectacles include rapper accompaniments like Eminem walking Terence Crawford, entertaining fans. Saudi promoters spend millions on arenas and entertainment entering, establishing as new powers.

Boxing appears entering a new era. Innovative strategies continue attracting new, casual fans, helping growth.

Despite changes over decades, boxing gives everything entertaining - storylines, fighters' perseverance.

Mixed martial arts' rising popularity posed boxing's biggest threat but lessons learned. Promotional tools seen in MMA now appear in boxing.

Boxing tests intelligence, skill, courage, determination through unique styles and endless matchups keeping fans engaged. Boxing's modern prominence showcases the enduring appeal of the sport. Exciting talent, thrilling matchups and innovative marketing is recapturing worldwide sports fans' imagination.

**The Big Four**. There are four major international sanctioning organizations in boxing: the World Boxing Council (WBC), World Boxing Association (WBA), International Boxing Federation (IBF), and World Boxing Organization (WBO). Each organization sanctions championship fights, with the winner granted the title of world champion and a championship belt.

As you know, this is why fighters may be referred to as, for example, the "WBC Champion" or "WBA Champion." If a fighter simultaneously holds belts from multiple but not all four sanctioning organizations, they are considered the "unified champion." Holding belts from all four organizations earns the distinction of "undisputed champion."

In the past, there were undisputed champions across multiple weight classes, such as Oleksandr Usyk in the cruiserweight division. As of 2024, the only undisputed champions in professional boxing are Terence Crawford and Naoya Inoue among men, and Katie Taylor and Clarissa Shields among women -- each having earned the title in two weight classes.

Every moment in the ring holds importance for boxers, whether competing for belts, medals or titles. Beyond the physical honors, boxers also fight for the passion and pride of the sport. Sanctioning organizations and promoters provide competitive opportunities that allow boxers to demonstrate their skills at the highest levels.

## Hagler v. Hearns -- Anticipation for an Epic Showdown

. On April 15, 1985, the boxing world eagerly awaited what was sure to be a historic middleweight title bout in Las Vegas.

Reigning undisputed champion Marvin Hagler was set to defend his belt against the formidable "Hitman" Tommy Hearns. Dubbed "The Fight," it promised to live up to its moniker and deliver all-out combat between two aggressive punchers.

Hagler came out swinging in the opening round, intent on setting a torrid pace from the outset against his normally fast-starting challenger. While Hearns was able to land a telling blow that opened a cut above Hagler's eye, the champion refused to be deterred. He kept up his relentless pressure to dominate the action.

By the second round, Hagler had closed the distance to minimize Hearns' reach advantage. He consistently worked the body to soften up his foe. Meanwhile, Hearns resorted to movement and boxing on the outside to stay clear of Hagler's powerful strikes. Hagler was undeterred in his quest for an all-out brawl.

All pretense of strategy vanished in the explosive third round. Hearns' offense had been blunted by Hagler's sustained punishment, while a broken right hand further hampered his effectiveness. Seizing the opportunity, Hagler uncorked a punishing overhand right that sent Hearns crashing to the canvas. Battered and beaten, Hearns bravely rose but was in no condition to continue, prompting the referee's intervention.

The war everyone anticipated was over, but it had surely lived up to its billing. Hagler emerged triumphant in one of boxing's most memorable rounds ever fought. An epic showdown for the ages was now etched in sports lore.

**Line up**. A reporter for the New York Gazette was doing some digging at a local boxing gym to get the scoop on why these places are such a big deal in the city. This gym in particular had quite the reputation for churning out some real bruisers, but no one could figure out their secret sauce.

Determined to get the straight dope, our intrepid journalist signed up for a class to see what all the fuss was about. Lo and behold, he wasn't the only rookie raring to rumble - some 30 other greenhorns showed up, ready to roll. They cooled their heels till Muscles McMountain, the human mountain who ran the joint, called them into the ring. "Alright maggots, let's see who's got the guts for a dust-up."

Our man found himself near the back of the pack, praying this was all just part of the hazing. But yikes - one by one, Muscles was laying them out! From jabs to hooks, each newbie got a knuckle sandwich till they stayed down. Blood and teeth flew as the herd thinned faster than expired milk. Sweating bullets, our boy knew his moment of truth was coming...and fast.

When it was finally his turn, the scribe had had enough. "Time out!" he yelled. "I'm not here to brawl, I'm just doing a story! Tell me what's really going on before you deck me too!"

Muscles grinned so wide you'd think his face would split. "It's simple really - the most important part of boxing is always, the punchline!"

## The Legendary Battle of Jack Dempsey vs. Luis Firpo.

On September 14, 1923, over 82,000 energetic boxing fans packed into the Polo Grounds stadium in New York City in anticipation of the heavyweight championship bout between title holder Jack Dempsey and ferocious challenger Luis Firpo.

Known as the "Wild Bull of the Pampas," Firpo had earned his reputation for his unrelenting aggression inside the ring. This highly anticipated clash was projected to be the second million-dollar gate in boxing history and did not disappoint in delivering non-stop, jaw-dropping action from the opening bell to the climactic conclusion.

As soon as the first round commenced, Firpo launched his assault, swinging powerfully in an attempt to take the champion's head off. He connected with a thunderous overhand right that sent the legendary Dempsey crashing to the canvas floor.

However, the resilient champion was back on his feet instantly, ready to retaliate. Over the next three minutes, these two warriors engaged in an astonishing exchange, trading knockdowns an incredible seven times between them before the bell.

In a moment that will be remembered forever in boxing lore, Firpo unleashed one final mammoth right hand that launched the great Dempsey completely over the top rope and out of the ring altogether. Alert ring attendants quickly pushed the still-groggy Dempsey back inside just before he could be counted out, saving him from a stunning first-round defeat.

As the second round began, the cunning Dempsey played possum, luring the charging bull Firpo into his trap. With lightning-fast counter hooks, the renowned "Manassa Mauler" found his opening and scored the picture-perfect knockout blow to successfully retain his title in dramatic highlight-reel fashion.

The roaring crowd of over 82,000 at the Polo Grounds was on their feet, witness to what is still regarded as perhaps the greatest prizefight of all time between two boxing legends. There is a YouTube video of this match referenced at the end of this book. [14]

**Boxing helps your mind**. The National Library of Medicine has reported a study that besides the exercise benefits, non-contact boxing provides a cathartic release of anger, aggression, stress, and the dissipation of anxious energy." [15]

Boxing also provides numerous mental health benefits in addition to its well-known physical advantages. While boxing transforms the body through fitness and strength gains, it also positively impacts the mind.

Boxing can help strengthen the mind in several keyways and described below. [16]

**Stress Relief** - Engaging in boxing involves a range of physical exertion from moderate to vigorous exercise. This physical activity stimulates the release of endorphins, helping to reduce stress and boost mood. Incorporating boxing into a lifestyle can effectively manage stress.

**Self-Awareness** - Boxing pushes limits and exposes strengths and weaknesses. Through this process, self-discovery occurs including better understanding of habits, beliefs, thought patterns, and personality traits.

**Self-Confidence** - Physical strength increases from boxing parallel mental empowerment. Developing a "fighter's spirit" imbues courage and morale, feeling empowered to accomplish goals.

**Anger Management** - Boxing provides an outlet to release tension and aggression through punching bags. It also shifts focus away from negative thoughts and emotions, helping anger dissipate.

**Sleep** - Boxing's moderate-vigorous activity and stress relief positively impact sleep quality by reducing time to fall asleep and time awake. Better sleep aids mental wellness by lowering depression and anxiety risk.

**Resilience** - Challenging boxing training strengthens the mind's fortitude. It cultivates focus and teaches practical defense skills while building confidence.

**Mindfulness** - Boxing facilitates present-moment focus similar to meditation. This rewards the mind by switching off stresses to concentrate solely on tasks.

**Emotional Regulation** - Focus requirements train the mind to pacify negative emotions and prioritize positive thinking, helping manage anger, anxiety, rumination and other unhelpful thoughts.

Overall, boxing maximizes mental well-being and strengths the mind in numerous impactful ways paralleling its renowned physical advantages. It effectively combats stress, cultivates self-awareness and confidence while facilitating anger management, quality sleep, resilience, mindfulness, and emotional regulation.

## The Title Fight of November 12th, 1982, in Miami.

It was time for Aaron "Hammer" Pryor to prove himself on the biggest stage. After Sugar Ray Leonard retired, Pryor would get his chance against legendary Alexis "El Flaco

Explosivo" Arguello. Arguello had already made history by winning titles in four divisions, but now sought Pryor's WBA Junior Welterweight belt.

From the opening bell, the fighters engaged in an intense battle. They unleashed rapid-fire punches and powerful shots in an instant classic matchup. Pryor relentlessly pressed forward with barrage after barrage. However, Arguello was also skilled, using his experience to maneuver and counter. Both withstood each other's strongest attacks in the furious exchange.

Round after grueling round, the intensity grew ever more violent. Though Arguello landed successfully as well, Pryor continued relentlessly. By the later rounds, both were exhausted but still throwing powerful punches. Pryor led on two judges' scorecards entering the championship rounds.

Then in the 14th, something seemed to change for Pryor as he exploded with renewed ferocity, battering Arguello until the referee stopped the fight. Arguello collapsed after the final bell in a stunning conclusion to the epic battle.

## Most Consecutive World Title Defenses in Boxing History.

Joe Louis was a legendary boxer who competed in the 20th century. With the nickname "Brown Bomber," Louis inspired many future heavyweight champions, such as Deontay Wilder, known as the "Bronze Bomber."

Joe captured the world heavyweight title at the young age of 23 in 1937, demonstrating his prowess in the ring. Perhaps most impressively, he defended the championship successfully in 26 consecutive bouts, a record that still stands today.

Dubbed an "unstoppable force" during his career, Joe exemplified excellence in the sport of boxing through his long reign as titleholder, highlighted by his unparalleled number of world title defenses over nearly a decade fighting the best opposition of his era. His historic accomplishment solidified his status as one of boxing's all-time greats.

**Frazier vs. Ali.** The 1971 Match. It was the battle boxing fans had been waiting years for - the undefeated heavyweights "Smokin'" Joe Frazier and "The Greatest" Muhammad Ali were set to finally settle the score in the biggest fight the world had ever seen!

On March 8th, 1971, Madison Square Garden was absolutely electric as over 20,000 frenzied fans packed the historic arena, with millions more tuning in worldwide.

With Ali looking for redemption after being stripped of his title for refusing the Vietnam draft and Frazier determined to prove he was the true champ, the intensity inside that ring was gonna be off the charts.

At that time, these guys straight up hated each other! Ali talked more trash than a garbage truck, but Frazier let his fists do the talking as the silent assassin. Their contrasting styles guaranteed an all-out war for the ages.

From the second the opening bell rang, it was an instant slugfest as neither man gave an inch. Ali tried using his famous speed, but Frazier was relentless, marching forward and lighting Ali up with thunderous hooks and uppercuts.

By the later rounds, Ali was gasping for air as the pressure never stopped. And in the epic 11th, Frazier landed a bomb of a left hook that nearly ended Ali for good! Somehow Ali hung on, but you could see the champ was fading fast.

In the end, it was Frazier's relentless pressure and dynamite power that proved too much, as he scored a massive knockdown in the 15th to secure the victory. While Ali tasted defeat for the first time, everyone knew this legendary rivalry was just getting started. An instant classic was cemented -- we could only imagine what insane battles still lied ahead!

His return bout with archrival Joe Frazier, dubbed "Super Fight II", took place at boxing's hallowed Madison Square Garden once more. Knowing Frazier's style of pressing forward, Ali trained fervently to keep moving.

Coming off grueling wins, Ali was primed with fast feet and elusiveness. He outboxed Frazier over twelve rounds, marking perhaps his final showcase of brilliant defensive dancing in the ring. "Super Fight II" remains one of boxing's most thrilling spectacles, as Ali solved the riddle of his greatest foe with masterful movement.

The final match of the trilogy was the "Thrilla in Manila." On October 1st, 1975, Ali and Frazier met in Manila, Philippines for their long-awaited rubber match. Dubbed "The Thrilla in Manila", this final battle between immortal rivals would not only settle the score once and for all, but cement their legacies as the two baddest men to ever do it.

Mirroring their first fight, Ali dominated the early rounds with his lightning hands and precision power shots. But no matter what Ali threw, Frazier's iron will refused to break as he marched forward throwing bombs.

By the middle rounds, Frazier had turned the tide, hammering Ali with punches that would shatter concrete. He took the lead on the cards through 11 rounds of all-out destruction.

Seeing his legacy on the line, Ali dug deeper than ever before, unloading a blistering barrage in the 13th and 14th that would've felled most men.

But despite Frazier's corner stopping the fight, he had earned immortality by battling Ali to the absolute limit of human endurance. "It was like death. Closest thing to dying that I know of," Ali said.

The Thrilla in Manila cemented their place among boxing's true immortals in the greatest trilogy the world had ever seen!

*Joe Frazier v. Muhammad Ali - Thrilla in Manila*

## What's your opinion on the greatest heavyweight ever?

Many say one of these five top heavyweights is the greatest. What do you think?

The heavyweight division in boxing is home to some of the most legendary athletes the sport has ever seen. These men were not only dominant champions in their era but also personalities that transcended the ring. Their unmatched power and skills have etched their names in the history books as the best big men to ever lace up the gloves. Here is a professional examination of the top 5 heavyweight champions of all time.

**Muhammad Ali** is widely considered the greatest boxer of all time. With his lightning-fast hands and feet along with an unrivaled charisma, Ali lived up to his self-proclaimed moniker of "The Greatest." He won the heavyweight title on three separate occasions, making him the only man to ever accomplish such a feat. Ali defeated Sonny Liston in 1964 to begin his historic run and went on to successfully defend his belts against top contenders like Joe Frazier, Ken Norton, and Floyd Patterson. His ability to overcome adversity both in and out of the ring solidified his legendary status.

Then there's **Rocky Marciano** who was the only heavyweight in history to retire with a perfect record, Rocky Marciano stands alone with his flawless mark of 49-0. What's more, an astonishing 43 of those wins came by way of knockout, earning Marciano the reputation as one of boxing's most feared punchers. After capturing the title from Jersey Joe Walcott in 1952, Marciano made an impressive 6 straight title defenses against top opposition. His relentless pressure style and thunderous power made "The Brockton Blockbuster" an undefeated champion.

What about **Joe Louis**? As the longest-reigning heavyweight king with over 11 years on top, "The Brown Bomber" Joe Louis holds the record for the most title defenses at 25. Louis knocked out contender Jim Braddock in 1937 to begin a legendary tenure in which he dominated the division for over a decade.

Louis took on all comers in an era overflowing with talent, besting legends like Max Schmeling, Billy Conn, and Jersey Joe Walcott. With 66 total wins and 52 knockouts, Louis left an undeniable mark as one of boxing's most dominant champions.

Some say **Larry Holmes**, with 21 successful title defenses over nearly a decade as champ, is one of the best. Nicknamed "The Easton Assassin," Holmes possessed pinpoint accuracy with his jab that he used to outpoint many talented opponents.

During his reign, Holmes defeated the likes of Ken Norton, Earnie Shavers, and Leon Spinks to cement himself as the top heavyweight of his era. Even after losing his title to Michael Spinks, Holmes continued fighting well into his 40s, showcasing the longevity of his hall of fame career.

Then there's **Tyson Fury** who has major accomplishments inside the ring. After becoming the first man to defeat Wladimir Klitschko in over a decade, Fury went on to add the lineal championship to his WBC and WBO belts.

So far in his career, Fury has amassed a 33-0-1 record while unifying the division and defeating notable foes like Derek Chisora, Otto Wallin, and Dillian Whyte. With his combination of size, athleticism, and mental toughness, Fury looks poised for more history as one of the great modern heavyweights.

## Sugar Ray Leonard v. Roberto Duran.
On April 6, 1975, in Montreal, "Sugar" Ray Leonard and Roberto "Manos de Piedra" Duran were considered the best boxers on the planet, and they finally met in Montreal.

Leonard was widely known for his technical abilities, and he was squaring off against Duran, the relentless aggressor.

Most everyone thought Leonard would be skillful and dancing but in a shocking twist, he decided to stand and trade bombs instead of letting his feet do the talking! They threw heavy for all 15 rounds. That was something that Leonard hadn't eve done before.

Duran came out like a tornado, ambushing Leonard from jump street. But the champ showed his warrior spirit by fighting fire with napalm against the aggressive Duran.

In round five, Leonard started to crack the code as he counterpunched Duran into next week. What followed was a back-and-forth barnstormer that had the packed house on their feet for most of the fight!

With so many razor close rounds, you just knew this one would go the all 15!

In the end, Duran's relentless pressure proved too much, as he edged out a razor thin unanimous decision in his favor.

In dethroning the great "Sugar" Ray Leonard, Duran had cemented himself as the king of the 147-pound division. Their incredible first encounter will forever be remembered as one of the all-time classic boxing slugfests!

*Sugar Ray Leonard and Roberto Duran*

**The biggest upset.** Most say the biggest professional upset in boxing was in the Mike Tyson vs. Buster Douglas in Tokyo. Going into the fight, Tyson was the undisputed heavyweight champion of the world and was very popular at the time. He held the WBC, WBA, and IBF titles.

Despite several controversies that marred Tyson's profile at the time, such as his allegedly abusive relationship and contractual battles between his longtime manager and promoter, as well as departing from his longtime trainer, Tyson was still dominant in the ring. He scored a 93-second knockout against Carl Williams in his previous fight, which most considered a warm-up bout for Tyson before meeting the then-undefeated number-one heavyweight contender Evander Holyfield.

Tyson was viewed as such a dominant champion that he was often considered the number-one fighter pound-for-pound, a rarity for heavyweights.

Buster Douglas was ranked as the #7 heavyweight contender and had met with mixed success in his professional career up to that point. His previous title fight resulted in a TKO in the 10th round. However, six consecutive wins since, including victories over a former world champion and future world champion, gave him the opportunity to fight Tyson.

In the time leading up to the fight, Douglas faced personal setbacks, including the death of his mother 23 days before the fight and his son's mother having a severe kidney ailment. He had also contracted the flu the day before the fight.

The HBO boxing analysts expected to see "another 90-second annihilation." Instead of discussing Douglas's chances, they compared their pets, Tyson had a white pit bull named "Duran" while Douglas had a beagle named "Shakespeare."

Singer Bobby Brown wrote in his autobiography that he met Tyson in Tokyo and the two partied extensively the night before the fight. Brown claims Tyson refused to go to sleep early for the fight, deeming Douglas "an amateur" he could beat even "if I didn't sleep for five weeks."

It was evident from the outset of the match that Douglas was unafraid. Douglas displayed nimble bodily movements and readily threw punches whenever opportunities arose to attack Tyson.

He adeptly utilized his quick and precise jab to prevent Tyson from closing the distance, where Tyson proved most formidable. When Tyson attempted to close in, Douglas would tie him up, retreat, or immediately strike Tyson with multiple blows as Tyson entered Douglas' range. Early on, Douglas exhibited greater agility than Tyson and out-landed Tyson in exchanges. Douglas finished the second round with a crisp uppercut to Tyson's chin.

Seeming to regain his form, Tyson delivered a punishing left blow to the body that gave Douglas pause to check in with his corner. After an ineffective and lackluster third round, Tyson's cornerman Jay Bright sternly instructed his fighter "Don't just stand there and look at him, you've gotta work!"

Boxing legend "Sugar" Ray Leonard, providing commentary for HBO at ringside, noted Douglas' dominance with the jab and right hand and observed Tyson experiencing one of those occasional matches in the ring where "you just don't have it...things just don't click in."

Douglas continued to hold sway through the middle rounds, though Tyson managed to land a few of his signature uppercuts. Tyson was stunned by a chopping right during the fifth round. Soon, Tyson's left eye began to swell from Douglas' right jabs, impeding his vision of his opponent's blows.

Tyson's cornermen were unprepared. They had neglected to bring an ice pack or ends well, typically standard equipment for a bout, so confident were they that Tyson would easily defeat Douglas.

Instead, they filled a rubber glove with ice water and held it on Tyson's eye between rounds. At one point, Aaron Snowell, Tyson's primary cornerman, inadvertently caught the chain from his identification badge between the iced glove and Tyson's injured eye. As Snowell moved, Tyson winced in pain as the chain dragged across his afflicted eye.

Confusion and panic grew in Tyson's corner as the match progressed. Despite Tyson's inability to execute an effective strategy, his corner persistently offered the same advice between rounds to move his head, lead with the jab, and follow with a right hand.

Within the last 10 seconds of the eighth round, Tyson, having been backed onto the ropes, landed a forceful right uppercut that sent Douglas to the canvas.

Though the knockdown timekeeper began the count as Douglas' backside touched the ring surface, reports indicate the referee independently started his count two beats behind. Douglas rose as the referee signaled nine, but the bell ended the round.

In evident frustration with his error, Douglas pounded his left fist on the mat. Tyson's promoter Don King would later argue unsuccessfully about the validity of the referee's count.

In the ninth round, Tyson came out aggressively seeking to end the fight and save his title, hoping Douglas remained weakened from the eighth-round knockdown. Douglas managed to withstand Tyson's onslaught and close Tyson's eye entirely.

Both men traded blows before Douglas connected with a four-punch combination that staggered Tyson back onto the ropes. With Tyson hurt along the ropes, Douglas bore in and unleashed a four-punch flurry aiming to knock Tyson out. Tyson endured the punishment and barely survived the ninth round.

In the tenth round, Tyson pushed forward, but he remained seriously damaged from the accumulated punishment absorbed throughout the bout. As Tyson advanced, Douglas measured him with a few jabs then landed an uppercut snapping Tyson's head upwards, halting Tyson's momentum. As Tyson reeled back, Douglas immediately followed with four head shots, dropping Tyson *for the first time in his career*.

In a famous scene, Tyson fumbled for his mouthguard on the canvas before awkwardly inserting one end in his mouth with the other end dangling out.

The champion strove to rise but referee Octavio Meyran counted him out. Buster Douglas thus became the new undisputed heavyweight champion, engineering one of the greatest upsets in boxing history. The official scorecards through nine rounds were 87–86 for Tyson, 86–86, and 88–83 for Douglas.

During the post-fight interview, Douglas broke down in tears when asked what enabled his victory when no one believed he could win. "Because of my mother, God bless her heart," said the emotional new champion.

*Buster Douglas*

## More about Health Benefits and Exercise.

Harvard Health reports boxing improves strength, endurance and balance. [17] The Cleveland Clinic has also reported the sport of boxing provides body and mind benefits since it is a form of high intensity interval training (HIIT). [18]

When used for fitness purposes, most boxing regimens avoid physical contact to minimize risks of injury, instead utilizing equipment like punching bags. Nonetheless, boxing continues to provide its inherent health benefits when practiced as an exercise routine.

Typical boxing fitness programs incorporate movement and footwork drills, as well as punching exercises using equipment such as heavy bags, speed bags, and focus mitts.

Virtual reality boxing systems utilizing motion sensors have also emerged. Additionally, many programs involve supplementary conditioning exercises such as rope jumping, calisthenics, and running.

Overall, boxing offers not only improved physical fitness but also presents a fun challenge for the mind and body. The following is a summary of key benefits.

**Enhanced Cardiovascular Health** - Boxing simulates high-intensity interval training, repeatedly sustaining intense exertion. This type of training reduces heart disease risk. Studies also link higher boxer rankings with better heart health markers.

**Aided Weight Management** - Boxing training decreases body fat and improves composition more than activities like brisk walking. A one-hour session can burn 390-558+ calories, varying by intensity and whether bag work or sparring is included.

**Augmented Whole-Body Strength** - Throwing punches engages the entire body from feet pushing off the ground to core and limb coordination. This comprehensive muscle engagement strengthens the entire system.

**Improved Balance** - Boxing's footwork, reactive movement, and strength building aid balance attributes. Studies find boxing programs strengthen balance, such as in stroke patients. It has also helped balance and fall risk for Parkinson's disease patients.

**Reduced Stress** - The cathartic release of punching aids stress relief. Most boxing regimens follow high-intensity interval protocols, which research links to mood enhancement.

**Lowered Blood Pressure** - Boxing and high-intensity interval training typically lower both systolic and diastolic pressure, reducing strain on the cardiovascular system. Direct comparisons show boxing superior to moderate exercise in this regard.

**Enhanced Endurance** - Traditional boxing prepares fighters for rounds lasting three minutes with one-minute rests. Fitness boxing drills similarly develop stamina.

**Positive Mental Health Impact**. Boxing drills provide a meditative focus while high-intensity interval training leaves little time for deep thought. Studies show boxing offers benefits such as a healthy outlet for emotions, better self-esteem and quality of life, reduced stress, and fewer anxiety/depression symptoms.

**Injury Prevention**. Proper form, gear, recovery, and listening to one's body can help prevent injuries when boxing.

Instructors teach safe techniques, and it is wise to consult a healthcare provider before beginning an intense new exercise program.

**Mental health**. Overall, boxing done safely and appropriately provides meaningful physical and mental health advantages.

Individuals of varying fitness levels can participate by selecting beginner-friendly classes and communicating needs to instructors. The empowerment of learning to box can also benefit one's confidence and resilience.

## The journey of Manny Pacquiao is truly inspirational.

Born into poverty in the slums of General Santos City in the Philippines, he rose from humble beginnings to become one of the greatest professional boxers of all time and one of the richest athletes in any sport.

Pacquiao's record in the ring is nothing short of astonishing. He is the only boxer in history to have won world titles in eight different weight classes, starting from flyweight at 112 pounds and working his way up to welterweight at 147 pounds. This unprecedented accomplishment is a testament to his dedication, hard work, and ability to continually challenge himself as his career progressed.

Another impressive feat is Pacquiao's longevity at the elite level. He is the only boxer in the history of the sweet science to have held a world championship in four separate decades. This speaks volumes about his elite level skills, champion mentality, and commitment to physical conditioning. His first world title came in 1998 in the flyweight division, and over 20 years later he won the WBA welterweight title in July 2019 before losing it in 2021 at the age of 42, having cemented his place as one of the sport's all-time greats.

*Manny Pacquiao*

**One for the ages!** On September 23rd, 1952, a boxing match took place at Municipal Stadium in Philadelphia, Pennsylvania. In front of over 40,000 energetic fans, 38-year-old Jersey Joe Walcott put his heavyweight championship of the world on the line against the formidable up-and-comer Rocky Marciano.

From the opening bell, it was obvious this contest was gonna be absolutely epic. Walcott, usually a technical boxer, came out swinging hard and dropped Marciano with a sweet left hook - the first time the durable Marciano had touched the canvas in his career. However, Marciano showed his championship mettle by bouncing back promptly and fighting ferociously to even things up.

Over the ensuing rounds, the two warriors engaged in an all-out war, trading massive blows in an incredible display of raw power and fortitude. Though Walcott drew first blood by opening a cut above Marciano's eye, the challenger gradually imposed his strength advantage. By rounds eleven and twelve, Marciano's sustained assault seemed to be wearing down the resilient titleholder.

As round thirteen began, it looked like the judges' scorecards might decide the victor. But Marciano was far from finished, and with under a minute left, he unleashed a massive overhand right that caught the fading Walcott leaning on the ropes. The thunderous punch echoed throughout the stadium as Walcott collapsed unconscious, forcing referee Charlie Daggert to halt the contest and crown Marciano as the new heavyweight king via knockout. Legendary boxing writer A.J. Liebling vividly described Walcott "flowing down like flour out of a chute" upon impact of Marciano's decisive blow.

The dramatic conclusion transformed Marciano into the premier fighter in the division. Fans demanded an immediate rematch between the new champion and his fallen predecessor, eager to see Marciano's reign unfold.

However, eight short months later, Marciano left no doubt who was the superior fighter by knocking Walcott out once more, this time in the opening round.

Rocky Marciano had taken the heavyweight crown and seemed poised to hold it for the foreseeable future. He held the world heavyweight championship from 1952 to 1956, during which time he remained undefeated. The six title defenses of his championship reign were against the following opponents, Jersey Joe Walcott (from whom he had won the title), Roland La Starza, Ezzard Charles (twice), Don Cockell and Archie Moore. He is the only heavyweight champion to hold his title undefeated.

*Rocky Marciano*

**Walks into a bar.** A tough guy walks into a bar, looking for trouble. Orders a boiler maker. He downs the shot, turns to the guy on his right and punches him in the face and says, "That's a right hook from boxing."

He drinks down the beer, turns to the guy on his left and kicks him in the belly. "That's a crane kick from Kung-fu."

He turns to see if anyone in the bar wants to fight. The bartender knocks him out with a blow from behind.

Bartender says, 'That's a tire iron from the Ford Motor Company!"

**Hagler vs. Sugar Ray Leonard.** After over half a decade in the making, these all-time greats finally went to war under the bright lights of Caesars Palace in a battle for the ages.

While Hagler had dominated the middleweight division for over a decade as the undisputed champ, racking up 12 straight title defenses, many thought Ray was washed up after being away from the ring for five long years. But they clearly didn't know Sugar Ray like they thought! The man was as fast and sharp as ever, having put in the work to get himself back in fighting form.

Through three action packed minutes, it was clear this was going to be an epic war for the history books! Leonard brought the speed and dancing that made him a star, while Hagler stalked him around the ring looking to land a thunderous hook to end the night early.

But Sugar Ray was too slick, using his angles and volume to steal rounds down the stretch so in the end, the judges scored it for Leonard by the slimmest of margins, handing Hagler his first ever loss in a career-defining upset.

While some say Hagler got robbed, you couldn't deny it was one of the fights of the decade! This classic battle cemented both men's legacies and left us all wanting more. Although talks of a rematch never came to be, we'll always have that night in Vegas to remember these legends going toe-to-toe in their prime.

## Most Punches Thrown in a Professional Boxing Match

Boxing is a sport defined by the throwing of punches between opponents. At its highest levels, world-class athletes leverage precise technique and immense physical conditioning to barrage their adversaries with powerful blows over the course of up to twelve grueling three-minute rounds.

Given the nature of the sport, it begs the question - just how many punches have been thrown in a single professional boxing match throughout history?

The answer to this question lies in a 2018 super welterweight bout between Jesus Soto Karass and Neeco Macias that took place in Phoenix, Arizona.

In what was an incredibly active and high-output contest, Soto Karass managed to establish a record that will be difficult to top, throwing a staggering 1,848 total punches over the course of their twelve-round clash.

Through relentless pressure and pace, Soto Karass was ultimately able to earn a majority decision victory on the judges' scorecards.

While boxing statistics and punch counts can often fail to capture the full drama and nuance of a fight, the sheer volume and relentlessness exhibited by Soto Karass in racking up nearly 1,850 punches thrown stands out as one of the most impressive and physically taxing performances in the long history of professional prizefighting.

It remains the standard for activity and work rate against which future punch output records will certainly be measured.

## A Historic Rivalry and Enduring Friendship.

The 1920s proved to be a golden age for American sports. Notable athletes like Jack Dempsey, Red Grange, and Babe Ruth achieved worldwide fame and acclaim. Heavyweight Champion, Jack "Manassa Mauler" Dempsey dominated his division until 1926, when Gene "The Fighting Marine" Tunney unexpectedly defeated him to claim the title.

Their highly anticipated rematch in the next year, 1927 was one for the record books. Held at Soldier Field in Chicago, the event drew over 104,000 spectators and grossed $2.6 million, both figures remain historic highs. Could the popular Dempsey regain his championship or would Tunney prove his initial victory was no fluke?

In a pivotal seventh round, Dempsey landed a powerful combination that knocked Tunney to the canvas for the first and only time in his career. However, Dempsey failed to immediately retreat to a neutral corner, granting Tunney additional recovery time according to some observers. Despite this controversial moment, Tunney demonstrated his toughness and composure by outboxing Dempsey over the final rounds to retain his title.

Though the crowd supported Dempsey, he later acknowledged Tunney's superiority, saying, "You were the best kid."

Despite their on-ring rivalry, Dempsey and Tunney developed a lifelong friendship, cementing their place in sports history through one of the most memorable athletic rivalries.

**Rope-a-Dope**. During the pinnacle of his storied boxing career, Muhammad Ali was renowned for his distinctive "rope-a-dope" tactical approach inside the ring.

This strategic maneuver employed by Ali was essentially a cunning bait and switch technique. Ali would purposefully portray vulnerability, motivating his adversaries to vigorously attack him while expending a tremendous amount of energy.

Remaining calm and composed against the ropes, Ali conserved his strength and stamina, allowing his opponents to aggressively throw punch after punch. Once Ali assessed that his rivals had expended nearly all of their reserves and were on the verge of exhaustion, he would spring into offensive action with precise and powerful counters.

Emerging from the ropes with a renewed vigor, Ali would then swiftly overwhelm and defeat his worn down and fatigued opponents. Through mental fortitude, cunning strategy and impeccable timing, Ali elevated the "rope-a-dope" maneuver into one of boxing's most iconic in-ring tactics.

**Rumble in the Jungle.** On October 30, 1974, in Kinshasa, Congo, Muhammad Ali demonstrated his elite skillset and fortitude in defeating George Foreman in their historic heavyweight bout, known as the Rumble in the Jungle.

Following his victory over Joe Frazier in their highly anticipated rematch, Ali was tasked with challenging the seemingly undefeatable heavyweight champion, George Foreman, who had obtained early victories over his prior opponents in a combined five rounds. The younger and undefeated Foreman was favored by most of the odds makers.

Ali maintained confidence and was determined to reclaim his title through exemplary performance.

Amidst the intense heat of Zaire, Ali and Foreman rigorously trained to acclimate to the environmental conditions. Considerable anticipation surrounded the event as the scheduled date approached. On the night of the fight, the stadium in Kinshasa was energized as the two renowned heavyweights finally competed under the bright lights.

Ali initiated the bout aggressively, evasively maneuvering around Foreman and launching punches to the head. However, Ali tactically shifted to his renowned "rope-a-dope" strategy, leaning against the ropes and enduring Foreman's powerful hooks. As Foreman intensified his offensive output, Ali maintained composure and conserved his stamina.

Ali impressively withstood blow after blow, demonstrating championship-level resilience. Yet his strategy was calculated - he discerned Foreman depleting his energy over successive rounds. In the eighth round, a fatigued Foreman exposed an opening, which Ali capitalized on with a lightning-quick counter to knock down Foreman, eliciting an elated response from spectators. Ali had once again achieved victory against formidable odds, reclaiming his title as heavyweight champion through formidable display. The bout reinforced Ali's premier skill and perseverance.

## Why is boxing called "The Sweet Science?"

The early study of boxing techniques and strategies was undertaken in 1747 by boxer John Godfrey through his published treatise entitled A Treatise Upon the Useful Science of Self Defense.

In this work, Godfrey put forth the hypothesis that combat skills, including those related to pugilism, appear to have innate foundations that can be observed even in infancy.

The renowned boxing author and journalist Pierce Egan coined the term "the sweet science" when referring to boxing as "the sweet science of bruising." Egan also reached the same conclusion as Godfrey years earlier - that fighting and thus boxing is an inherent, innate instinct ingrained in our DNA.

In his series of boxing articles titled Boxiana, Egan observed resentment some individuals felt growing up. They felt society had slighted them, and as a result this resentment would manifest as a necessary means of physical retribution. However, through evolution, modern man was able to restrain his "coolness, checking the fiery passion and rage" which differed from ancestors before, free from primitive actions, thereby forming boxing into this "sweet science."

Finally, in 1949 boxer/author A.J. Liebling introduced the term into modern times and credited Egan. In his novel The Sweet Science, Liebling writes about boxing's golden era and the science of boxing as a way of life.

While Godfrey and Egan made compelling arguments for boxing's actual scientific underpinnings and its relation to inherited nature, Liebling took a more contemporary approach to the "sweet science" and its present-day perception.

One example of the "sweet science of boxing" Liebling depicted was the 1955 heavyweight title fight between Archie Moore vs. Rocky Marciano. Liebling described the fighters' styles leading up to the fight. He viewed Marciano's style as inherently "natural" and said he needn't worry about defense as it might "spoil his natural prehistoric style."

When discussing Moore, Liebling portrayed his style as "nurtured," relying on craftsmanship and intellect versus Marciano's more savage approach. However, Marciano ultimately prevailed. It was this deeper examination of the "science" behind fighters as a modern concept that cemented the term's present-day usage relating to boxing's art form, fighting styles, and preparation.

Today boxers must not only be innately savage but also methodical, tactical, cunning and scientific. Muhammad Ali, arguably boxing's greatest, epitomized the sport's science. Even before fights he would psychologically manipulate opponents, trash-talking to sow doubt. As a result, many entered the ring already doubting themselves, usually to Ali's benefit.

Another classic example was Ali's "rope-a-dope" to defeat heavy favorite George Foreman in the Rumble in the Jungle. Foreman tired punching Ali's defensive posture against the ropes, and Ali knocked him out in round eight regaining his championship title.

Other boxers have also leveraged the "sweet science." Floyd Mayweather Jr., perhaps the best defensive fighter ever at 50-0, meticulously gauges opponents' strengths and weaknesses over early rounds. He surgically dissects them mid-fight to his advantage.

Lennox Lewis said, "In boxing, you create a strategy to beat each new opponent, it's just like chess." Truly an art form, the strategic "chess match" between boxers far surpasses wild swinging - finesse, cunning, swagger and art define the essence of boxing as both science and sweet.

*Lennox Lewis*

**The longest boxing match.** The Guinness World Record for the longest professional boxing match is 7 hours and 19 minutes. Andrew Bowen was an American lightweight boxer who is best known for participating in the world's longest boxing match in 1893 against Jack Burke.

Bowen's first fight was in 1887. He was undefeated in his first 14 fights, winning 12 and drawing two. In September 1890, he successfully defended his title against Jimmy Carroll at the Olympic Club in New Orleans (the same club where James J. Corbett would later defeat John L. Sullivan for the World Heavyweight Championship two years later).

The long fight took place on April 6, 1893, when Bowen and Jack Burke fought the longest fight in history.

Bowen had originally scheduled the fight with another opponent, however after the opponent withdrew, Jack Burke, who was the latter's trainer, fought the bout instead.

The fight lasted 110 rounds over seven hours and 19 minutes (each round lasting three minutes). Reports state the spectators who stayed to watch the fight had fallen asleep in their seats due to the lengthy duration.

It was also recorded that by round 108, with no clear resolution in sight, referee John Duffy decided that if a winner had not emerged in the next 2 rounds, the bout would be ruled a "no contest". With both men having become too dazed and too tired to return to their corners, Duffy declared the match a no contest.

Burke broke all the bones in both of his hands and was bedridden for six weeks. He had considered retiring after the fight but chose to continue competing.

**From rags to riches.** Manny Pacquiao's journey serves as an inspiration to many. Born into poverty in the slums of General Santos City, Philippines, Pacquiao rose from humble beginnings to become one of the most accomplished boxers in history and one of the highest-paid athletes worldwide.

Pacquiao's record in the boxing ring is nothing short of astonishing. He remains the only boxer in history to win world titles in eight different weight divisions, starting from flyweight at 112 pounds up to welterweight at 147 pounds. This unprecedented accomplishment underscores Pacquiao's remarkable skill, discipline, and determination in continually moving up in weight class while maintaining championship-caliber performance.

Another testament to Pacquiao's boxing greatness is his distinction as the only boxer to be a world champion in four separate decades. He first captured a flyweight title in 1998 and as recently as 2019 added the WBA welterweight belt to his collection before relinquishing it in 2021. This longevity of championship tenure over more than two decades against ever-evolving competition stands as one of boxing's most impressive feats.

Manny Pacquiao's rise from poverty-stricken origins to elite global athlete and recognition as among history's best pound-for-pound fighters serves as an inspiration and a testament to human potential through relentless hard work, commitment to excellence, and refusal to accept limitations.

According to the respected business publication Forbes, Manny Pacquiao was identified as the equal sixth highest paid athlete in the world for the period spanning late 2008 through mid-2009. [19]

During this six-month window, Pacquiao's total earnings amounted to $40 million United States dollars, which converts to approximately 2 billion Philippine pesos.

Tied with Pacquiao for the sixth position on Forbes' ranking was professional basketball player LeBron James of the National Basketball Association as well as champion golfer Phil Mickelson. All three athletes generated $40 million in income within the stated time frame, sharing the number six spot on Forbes' prestigious listing of highest compensated competitors across global sports.

*Manny Pacquiao*

**The Brown Bomber.** The 22nd of June in the year 1938 was destined to be an eventful evening at the famous Yankee Stadium in New York City! The highest honor in pugilistic endeavors, the heavyweight championship of the world, was to be defended on this night as America's own "Brown Bomber", Joe Louis, was matched against Max Schmeling of Germany in a historic revival of their previous confrontation.

But this prize fight signified far more than a mere test of boxing skill, for the tensions of a world on the precipice of war had infiltrated between the ropes. Schmeling had emerged as a champion of the German Reich following his astonishing victory over Louis two years prior.

Now, Louis sought retribution while carrying the hopes and aspirations of all Americans. Over seventy thousand spectators packed the stadium with millions more following the clash worldwide through radio broadcasts. Indeed, this proved to be a momentous clash that would reverberate around the globe!

From the commencement of hostilities, Louis emerged like a force of nature, pursuing a conclusive end to proceedings. He was not to allow a repetition of their last encounter. Schmeling attempted to employ his seasoned guile to weary Louis, but the Brown Bomber would tolerate none of it. After a brief feeling out of each other's strengths, pandemonium erupted as Louis unleashed himself giving Schmeling tremendous volleys. Schmeling was stunned by Louis' newfound might and precision.

Though the German fought valiantly, it soon became evident this evening belonged to the Brown Bomber. With a perfectly placed right hand, Louis sent Schmeling to the canvas and the stadium erupted in cheers!

Schmeling arose but was met with a barrage that toppled him twice more, ending the contest. America had found its new champion and a message was delivered around the world - this was Joe Louis' era! The Brown Bomber had ignited a spark for a new age in heavyweight pugilism and beyond.

*Joe Louis*

**An Interesting fact about George Foreman.** One of the greatest heavyweight boxers of his era was George Foreman, who as you know, famously fought Muhammad Ali in the 1974 bout known as "The Rumble in the Jungle." As one of the premier athletes of the 1960s, Foreman earned high purses commensurate with his status as a champion pugilist.

Surprisingly, George Foreman found even greater financial achievement as an entrepreneur later in life. He endorsed and lent his name to a dual-sided electric grill that has since become ubiquitous in homes worldwide.

Over 100 million units of the George Foreman Grill have been sold, generating hundreds of millions in royalties from use of his branding.

The earnings derived from this entrepreneurial endeavor far surpassed Foreman's career earnings from his time competing in the ring.

*George Foreman v. Muhammad Ali*

**The Bite Fight.** The match began with Evander Holyfield dominating Mike Tyson. Holyfield won the first three rounds.

In the first round, at the 2 minute and 19 second mark, Holyfield stunned Tyson with an overhand right punch. However, Tyson fought back immediately by pushing Holyfield backwards.

Then early in the second round, Holyfield ducked under a right punch from Tyson. In doing so, he head-butted Tyson, producing a large cut over Tyson's right eye. Tyson had repeatedly complained about head-butting in their first bout. Upon reviewing replays, referee Mills Lane determined that the headbutts were unintentional and not punishable.

As the third round was about to begin, Tyson exited his corner without his mouthpiece. Lane ordered Tyson back to his corner to insert it. Tyson inserted his mouthpiece and resumed the match.

Tyson began the third round with a furious attack. With forty seconds remaining in the round, Holyfield got Tyson in a clinch. Tyson then rolled his head above Holyfield's shoulder and bit Holyfield on his right ear, tearing off a *one-inch* piece of cartilage which Tyson spat out onto the ring apron.

Holyfield leapt into the air in pain and spun in a circle, bleeding profusely from the bite wound. Lane stopped the action. However, Tyson managed to rush Holyfield from behind and shove him into his corner before Lane separated the men. Lane moved Tyson to a neutral corner and checked on the enraged

Holyfield. The fight was delayed for the next few minutes as Lane decided how to proceed.

Lane informed Marc Ratner, the chairman of Nevada's athletic commission, of the situation. Lane stated that because Tyson had bitten Holyfield's ear, he intended to disqualify Tyson and end the fight. However, Lane first deferred to ringside physician Flip Homansky, who cleared Holyfield to continue fighting. As a result, Lane allowed the bout to continue but penalized Tyson with a two-point deduction for the intentional foul causing injury, per the rules.

When Lane explained the decision to Tyson and his cornermen, Tyson claimed that Holyfield's ear injury was the result of a punch. Lane retorted "Bull#!%t."

During another clinch, Tyson bit Holyfield's left ear. Holyfield threw his hands around to escape the clinch and jumped back, with Tyson only scaring Holyfield's ear with the second bite.

At the time of the second bite, Lane did not stop the match and both fighters continued until time expired. However, when the second bite was discovered afterwards, the match was halted again.

Holyfield stopped Tyson after 11 rounds, but it was the referee who officially called the fight as Tyson was rightly disqualified for biting Holyfield. Tyson lost his license to fight in Nevada and paid a fine of $3 million. After appeal, Tyson regained his license about a year later in 1998..

Tyson later opened up about the infamous match on The Oprah Winfrey Show in 2009. Tyson revealed that at the time, he felt no remorse and was not genuinely apologetic in his earlier public apology. Rather, he said he felt pressured into apologizing by the reaction to biting Holyfield. Tyson disclosed that he was annoyed by Holyfield's superior performance and wanted to inflict pain on him to gain an advantage.

In an incredible moment, Holyfield joined Tyson on the set of The Oprah Winfrey Show. For the first time, Tyson gave a genuine apology directly to Holyfield for his actions during their 1997 bout. Speaking to Holyfield, Tyson said "This is a beautiful man. We watched each other grow to become esteemed fighters. It's been a pleasure passing through life with you."

The two former rivals finally buried the hatchet after over a decade, with Tyson rightly making amends for one of the darkest moments of his career in an unforgettable television moment.

**Quick KOs**. Here are accounts of some remarkably fast knockouts in men's boxing history. Gerald "G-Man" McClellan required minimal time to defend his WBC World Middleweight Title against Jay Bell in 1993, landing a picture-perfect body shot to Bell's liver that caused him to collapse in just 20 seconds.

Power puncher David "Tuaman" Tua also made a name for himself in the 1990s through his swift finishing abilities. In 1996 against John Ruiz, Tua carefully measured the distance before unleashing a thunderous left hook that disrupted Ruiz's balance. Tua then capitalized to end the fight in a mere 19 seconds with nine additional punches.

Daniel "La Cobra" Jimenez stunned the home crowd watching Harald Geier in Austria in 1994. All that was needed was a single strike - a 17 second knockout.

Zolani Tete's 2017 defeat of Siboniso Gonya in Belfast, Northern Ireland earned Tete the WBO Bantamweight Title in the second fastest men's knockout ever at a swift 11 seconds. A powerful right hand found its mark cleanly on Gonya's chin as he leaned in -- *the very first punch of the bout*.

The record for the most rapidly achieved male knockout belongs to Phil "Drill" Williams, who dispatched Brandon Burke in a mere 10 seconds in 2007. Burke charged in recklessly only to pay dearly with a vicious right hook from Williams that left him face down, unable to beat the count. The right precision and power can end a fight in the blink of an eye.

However, in all of boxing, the fastest knockout appears to be a women's match when Seniesa Estrada took seven seconds to knock out Miranda Adkins in their bout. Check out the YouTube referenced in the endnotes of this book. [20]

## Mike Tyson's Near Encounter With a Gorilla.

Mike Tyson is well known for his fearsome reputation in the ring, but little known is an event from earlier in his career that demonstrated another side of his character.

According to reports, in the 1980s Tyson rented out an entire zoo for a private evening. As he toured the facilities, he came upon the gorilla enclosure. There he observed dominance behaviors between the primates that disturbed him. One large male gorilla, or silverback, was observed bullying the other, weaker gorillas in the group.

Witnessing this dynamic unfold before him, Tyson impulsively offered the zookeeper a sum of $10,000 to open the enclosure, with the goal of intervening in the situation himself. By his own account, he wished to "address the aggressive behavior of the silverback directly."

Fortunately for all parties involved, especially the gorillas, the zookeeper declined the offer, recognizing the risks involved in such an encounter.

While unconventional, some say this story provides a glimpse into Tyson's willingness to take swift action to defend those he saw as being mistreated or bullied. It serves as a reminder of the complexity of even famously fierce individuals.

## Riddick Bowe v. Andrew Golota -- Strange match. In early 1996, Riddick Bowe sought to regain

contention for the world heavyweight championship title. Since losing his World Boxing Association and International Boxing Federation championships to Evander Holyfield in their second fight, Bowe had participated in five comeback bouts, winning four with one no-contest against Buster Mathis, Jr.

He also defeated Herbie Hide for the then-fringe World Boxing Organization heavyweight title, making one successful defense before vacating to challenge Holyfield for a third time in November 1995, winning via technical knockout in the eighth round.

Meanwhile, a former rival of Bowe's also aimed to return to title consideration. After Bowe defeated Holyfield in their first 1992 bout to claim the undisputed world heavyweight championship, the World Boxing Council ordered him to make a mandatory defense against Lennox Lewis, who bested Bowe at the Olympics four years prior to win the super heavyweight gold medal.

Bowe declined and relinquished the WBC belt, symbolically depositing it in the trash.

Lewis held the title until September 1994 when Oliver McCall controversially knocked him out. McCall made one successful defense against former champion Larry Holmes but lost his next to Lewis' countryman Frank Bruno.

Per the terms negotiated by McCall's promoter Don King, Bruno had to immediately defend the WBC title against former undisputed champion Mike Tyson, another King client. Lewis sued unsuccessfully to cancel the bout and compel Bruno, whom he previously defeated via technical knockout in 1993, to defend against him as number one contender. In only his third fight after release from prison, Tyson knocked out Bruno on March 16, 1996, to regain the WBC title, making Lewis his mandatory challenger.

Concurrently, Tyson and King pursued a title unification match with WBA champion Bruce Seldon, who won the belt in April 1995 against former titleholder Tony Tucker after George Foreman was stripped for refusing to fight Tucker. Tyson and Lewis' camps agreed to allow Tyson to face Seldon first, leaving Lewis to seek a new opponent. Lewis and Bowe finally agreed to their long-awaited bout, tentatively scheduled for fall 1996.

Prior to then, Lewis and Bowe each accepted tune-up fights on HBO. Lewis won his May 10, 1996, against former WBO champion Ray Mercer via a disputed majority decision at Madison Square Garden.

Bowe opted to challenge undefeated Polish heavyweight Andrew Golota, the 1988 bronze medalist who earned most victories by knockout but lacked big name opposition. Golota was also notorious for frequent fouling during matches, including biting Samson Po'uha on the neck.

Ahead of their bout, the confident Bowe dubbed himself "The People's Champion" and paid little mind to Golota, looking past him toward Lewis and a potential super fight with Tyson.

Though entering at a career-high 252 pounds, 12 pounds heavier than his previous Holyfield match, Bowe remained a

12-1 favorite. Explaining his weight gain, Bowe made clear he had not trained much for Golota, infamously asking "How do you train for a bum?"

Golota's trainer Lou Duva remained optimistic his fighter could upset Bowe, commenting on Bowe's weight gain: "He's everything I want him to be."

In the opening round, Golota took advantage of Bowe being overweight and came out firing forcefully. Golota was able to land his jab at a consistent rate and landed nearly half of his 69 punches in the first round while Bowe was only able to land 17.

The two men would have a close round 2 with both men landing powerful shots on one another, but Golota regained control in round 3 and pushed the action further in round 4. Bowe was looking overmatched and an upset was becoming more likely for the Polish contender as the fight progressed. Bowe did not have an answer for Golota and was clearly out of shape and struggling as the fight advanced into the middle rounds.

Golota, however, was unable to refrain from his habit of committing infractions against his opponents. He had been landing punches to Bowe's midsection that were dangerously close to his belt line for much of the earlier portions of the fight, and eventually hit Bowe in his left thigh to garner his first warning from Kelly in the second round.

A second warning came after a punch from Golota hit Bowe in his crotch later in the round. Then, in the third round, Golota landed another low shot to Bowe's crotch that was forceful enough to send the former world champion to the canvas. Kelly took a point away from Golota and allowed Bowe five minutes to recover. After three minutes, Bowe was recovered and the fight resumed.

The seventh round began with Golota continuing to press the action, but he again managed to hit Bowe with a low blow. Kelly again stopped the action to deduct a point from Golota and allow Bowe a chance to recover, but warned Golota that he would stop the fight if he did it one more time.

Golota acknowledged the warning, but a few moments later he hit Bowe with two more shots to his crotch. After the second shot, which sent Bowe to the canvas again, Kelly disqualified Golota.

Immediately after the fight was stopped, members of Bowe's security team entered the ring and approached Golota, who had his back turned as he was going back to his corner. One of the men pushed Golota from behind which caused Golota to respond by throwing punches at the man. Another man, later identified as Jason Harris, began hitting Golota in the head with a walkie-talkie, opening up a cut that required 11 stitches to close.

Golota's trainer, 74-year-old Lou Duva, was also injured in the melee and collapsed to the canvas after experiencing chest pains and ultimately had to be taken from the ring on a stretcher.

*Trainer Lou Duva*

Eventually, fans of both boxers entered the brawl and would continue to trade punches with each other and the entourages inside the ring as well as outside of it.

Sky Sports announcers Ian Darke and Glenn McCrory merely ducked at ringside for their own protection, with Darke also making mention of beverage cups being thrown from the balconies of the venue.

The HBO announcers were more active in the situation, as the riot's dismantling of the HBO announcers' table prompted commentator Jim Lampley to move up a couple levels of Madison Square Garden while his colleagues Larry Merchant and George Foreman stayed at ringside.

Foreman even tried to stop the riot in the ring himself by saving Lampley and Merchant from fans attacking them, as well as discouraging other fans from entering the ring and attacking anyone.

The scene that followed referee Kelly's ruling marked an ugly end to what had been a much-hyped boxing match at one of the sport's most storied venues. It was as the ending credits began to roll on the HBO telecast that the police were finally shown arriving at the scene to make apprehensions. In the end, 10 arrests were made, eight officers were injured and nine spectators had to be hospitalized.

*Andrew Golota*

## The Evolution and Future of Boxing.

As mentioned, the sport of boxing has a long and storied history that has undergone significant changes over time.

Virtual and augmented reality platforms have the potential to transform fighter preparation. Boxers may train virtually by engaging in realistic simulated bouts or reviewing past performances from a first-person perspective. Such immersive training techniques could fundamentally change fighting styles through strategic scenario analysis and skills development in a safe environment.

Biometric sensors incorporated into equipment may also track vital signs during competition, so coaches are able to continuously monitor athlete health and performance in real-time.

Cutting-edge analytics tools could further provide deep statistical insights into variables like strike combinations, speed, and accuracy to optimize game planning.

Ongoing discussions regarding headgear and new weight classification standards indicate regulatory bodies' focus on short and long-term athlete well-being. Potential reforms may reevaluate protective gear requirements or impose stricter penalties for risky weight cutting behaviors through enhanced monitoring.

Women's boxing is expanding. As the popularity of women's boxing continues expanding, expectations are that dedicated divisions, marquee matchups, and greater representation will follow.

Likewise, heightened globalization may introduce breakout stars from previously underserved regions. Organizations may also facilitate smoother amateur-to-pro transitions through structured development pipelines and financial incentives.

Manufacturers face pressure to adopt eco-friendly materials and practices. Promoters have an opportunity to "green" event operations as environmental consciousness increases. Fans stand to further engage through virtual reality broadcasts and real-time interactive betting integrated into the live viewing experience.

Boxing's future appears bright -- evolving through regulatory changes emphasizing athlete welfare, technological innovations enhancing training and safety, diverse international talent, and adaptations ensuring the sport's environmental sustainability and exciting fan engagement for generations to come.

As a timeless and captivating form of entertainment, boxing most likely will maintain its place in sports history by creatively responding to a rapidly changing world.

*Ring Revelations*
*Unraveling the Mysteries of Boxing's Past, Present, and Future*

## We hope you enjoyed the book!

Thank you for reading! If you liked the book, we would sincerely appreciate your taking a few moments to leave a review.

Thank you again very much!

Bruce Miller

## About the author.

**Bruce Miller**. Bruce Miller is an award-winning author and boxing enthusiast. As an attorney and businessman, he has achieved success in multiple career paths. However, Mr. Miller's passion lies in continuous learning and sharing knowledge. He spends his days studying, writing, and exploring the ever-changing world around us.

Mr. Miller has written over 50 books in various genres. Several of his works have become bestsellers. In addition to his literary works, Mr. Miller is also an aviator and active member of several professional organizations related to his interests.

# We Want to Hear from You!

*"There usually is a way to do things better and there is opportunity when you find it."* - Thomas Edison

We love to hear your thoughts and suggestions on anything and please feel free to contact me at bruce@teamgolfwell.com

## Other Books by Bruce Miller

*Beware the Ides of March: A Novel Based on Psychic Readings (Awarded Distinguished Favorite by the NYC Big Book Award 2023).*

*The Book of Unusual Sports Knowledge.*

*Guy Wilson Creating Golf Excellence: The Genesis of Lydia Ko & More Stars.*

*For a Great Fisherman Who Has Everything: A Funny Book for Fishermen.*

*For the Golfer Who Has Everything: A Funny Golf Book.*

*For a Tennis Player Who Has Everything: A Funny Tennis Book.*

*The Funniest Quotations to Brighten Every Day: Brilliant, Inspiring, and Hilarious Thoughts from Great Minds.*

*For Bright Legal Minds Who Have It All.*

*And many more…*

# References

[1] Onomastus of Smyrna, Wikipedia, , Wikipedia, https://en.wikipedia.org/wiki/Onomastus_of_Smyrna
[2] Billy Bird, Wikipedia, https://en.wikipedia.org/wiki/Billy_Bird
[3] Ibid.
[4] Len Wickwar, Wikipedia, https://en.wikipedia.org/wiki/Len_Wickwar
[5] Len Wickwar, Wikipedia, https://en.wikipedia.org/wiki/Len_Wickwar
[6] Mike Tyson, Britannica, https://www.britannica.com/biography/Mike-Tyson
[7] Floyd Mayweather, Jr., Wikipedia, https://en.wikipedia.org/wiki/Floyd_Mayweather_Jr. https://en.wikipedia.org/wiki/Floyd_Mayweather_Jr.
[8] Sugar Ray Robinson, Wikipedia, https://en.wikipedia.org/wiki/Sugar_Ray_Robinson#Jimmy_Doyle_incident
[9] Steve Ward, Wikipedia, https://en.wikipedia.org/wiki/Steve_Ward_(boxer)
[10] Bernard Hopkins, Wikipedia, https://en.wikipedia.org/wiki/Bernard_Hopkins#Professional_boxing_record
[11] Nipper Pat Daly, Wikipedia, https://en.wikipedia.org/wiki/Nipper_Pat_Daly
[12] Ibid.
[13] Gervonta Davis vs. Ryan Garcia, Wikipedia, https://en.wikipedia.org/wiki/Gervonta_Davis_vs._Ryan_Garcia
[14] Jack Dempsey vs Luis Angel Firpo (Sept 1923), YouTube, https://www.youtube.com/watch?v=9NN0vGHnCLo

[15] Boxing as an Intervention in Mental Health: A Scoping Review, NIH National Library of Medicine, https://www.ncbi.nlm.nih.gov/pmc/articles/PMC10328201/
[16] Ibid.
[17] Punch Up Your Exercise Routine With Fitness Boxing, Harvard Health, https://www.health.harvard.edu/exercise-and-fitness/punch-up-your-exercise-routine-with-fitness-boxing
[18] Six Health Benefits of Boxing, Cleveland Clinic, https://health.clevelandclinic.org/benefits-of-boxing
[19] The World's Highest-Paid Athletes (2009) – Archived August 5, 2017, at the Wayback Machine. Forbes.com (June 17, 2009). Retrieved on May 19, 2012.
[20] Seniesa Estrada KOs Miranda Adkins In SEVEN Seconds, YouTube, https://www.youtube.com/watch?v=OKEdGAdO2J0